THE VANISHING LAND

THE VANISHING LAND

The Corporate Theft of America

FRANK BROWNING

HARPER COLOPHON BOOKS
Harper & Row, Publishers
New York, Evanston, San Francisco, London

Designed by Eve Callahan

First HARPER COLOPHON edition published 1975.

LIBRARY OF CONGRESS CATALOG CARD NUMBER: 75-782

STANDARD BOOK NUMBER: 06-090361-9

75 76 77 78 79 80 10 9 8 7 6 5 4 3 2 1

Contents

Acknowledgments

Among those who have been helpful in providing research and criticism for this book are Bruce Lovelett, Victor Reinemer, Susan Sechler, Steve Weissman, Patsy Truxaw, and the Agribusiness Accountability Project of Washington, D. C. Special appreciation is extended to Howard Bray, Joan Daves, and Hugh Van Dusen. Responsibility for any errors of fact or interpretation is solely the author's.

Research for this book was conducted with the help of a grant from the Fund for Investigative Journalism, Washington, D. C.

Portions of the book have appeared in *Ramparts* and *The New York Times*.

1

This Land Is Their Land

When some 200 years ago a real estate speculator named Daniel Boone slashed his way to the top of the Cumberland in the middle of the Appalachians, he saw blanketed before him the largest territorial commons in the history of North America. He stood dumb, it is said, silently dipping his imagination into the future far enough to see those grasslands completely filled with commerce. The land, then as now, was called Kentucky, and for centuries it had been communally shared among the Shawnee, the Cherokee, and the Delaware Indians as a source of fine hunting, fishing, and seasonal agriculture.

Two hundred years later Kentucky is once again on the verge of the land peddler's dream. Caught up in the nation's headlong lust for land, the state is faced with a real estate hustle nearly as profound as the one Boone and his fellow settlers first unleashed. The fight over land in the Bourbon state is just as vital to Americans in Maine or New Mexico as it is to the small tillers who scratch out a living along the banks of the Kentucky and Ohio Rivers, farmers who because of their number and obligation to their own communities, resemble the ideal of dispersed, independent Jeffersonian democrats as nearly as have any people in America's past. In their fight against the subdividers and the professional recreationists, they are raising one of the fundamental political, ecological, and cultural issues of the century: Who shall use the land and for what purposes?

Today farming in Kentucky is not principally a tax shelter for doctors, public officials, and lawyers grown obese from lofty incomes. Neither the pastures nor the people resemble the company *latifundia* of Texas or California. The farms are small, family owned, and almost universally they are the only source of income for the people who work them. Nationally, such farms are disappearing at the rate of over 1,000 per week, their death rattles smothered by the clanging cash registers of shopping malls, suburban tracts, and fantasmagorical recreation parks.

The speculators in Kentucky's soil have found a classic rallying point in the construction of a new international jetport for Louisville, Kentucky's largest city. When they failed in a key bid for the 1972 Democratic National Convention, the state's realtors, Louisville's Chamber of Commerce, and a suave collection of greater Louisville's *crème de la crème* concocted a scheme to replumb the state's economy as the Miami Beach of the lower Midwest, a genteel, aristocratic mirror to Mayor Daley's Convention City, it's pinion two sleek ribbons of runway and a control tower designed along the lines of a wax-sealed bottle of Maker's Mark. Farming, they proclaimed, was a dying business, threatening that if the state's taxpayers knew what was good for them, they would take whatever commercial future the developers chose to offer. That, of course, is why the airport's dreamers determined to locate well beyond suburban Louisville in one of three rural counties, thereby gobbling up hundreds of acres of fine crop and dairy land—cheap. From the airport would come growth: hotels, shopping malls, amusement parks, new towns, freeways. All the ambrosia of Miami and Ft. Lauderdale, but with sourmash stills lurking back beneath the spreading oaks. Among themselves the developers came to call this new future the Golden Triangle; it was to cover all of northern Kentucky from Louisville over to Lexington's horse farms and race tracks, then up to Cincinnati and the Ohio River.

The dimwitted feudal farmers, however, did not seem enthusiastic about turning their sowlots into shopping centers. Aided by poet-farmer Wendell Berry, the gentle country people banded together into an organization called Save Our Land to say "No!" "The redcoats are coming," Berry warned in newspaper articles, and his friends and neighbors came in droves to public hearings and wrote letters to local papers protesting the threatened loss of land and livelihood. "I've got seven and a half acres," one man explained at a meeting in a country Baptist church. "From what I can tell, they want to take every inch of it. I bought it for a home for the rest of my life, but it seems to me the [Greater Louisville] Air Board had different plans for me." To the surprise of the developers such little farmers started winning; none of the counties would support the Air Board or its backers or recognize their claim of eminent domain; when the issue rose to the Statehouse in Frankfort, even the governor feared to support the developers' campaign.

The case for rural survival and independence in Kentucky is no different from similar arguments all over America. Farmers and rural activists from every part of the United States have just in recent years begun to declare themselves unexpendable, insisting that the alternative to the struggling small farm is neither Tenneco's vast estates nor Walt Disney's dream of a pavement Fantasyland. They argue that America will have lost something vital to its best hopes for freedom and democracy if farming and fun are all supplied by ITT and Chrysler and Southern Pacific and Greyhound and the Peabody Coal Company in one great Gold Rush for land.

For America's grand corporate conglomerates land is an ideal investment. It supplies steady cash, a solid if not spectacular earnings profile, and when undertaken through massive capital syndicates, one of the friendliest tax loss programs the government has ever offered. To see what the Gold Rush means concretely, one only need turn to California. There ten corporations own over 12 percent of all private land in the state—topped off by the ubiquitous trails of the Southern Pacific Railroad. And there are more dirt gamblers in the Golden State than Las Vegas has ever seen on a Labor Day weekend, gathering up tens of thousands of acres to be auctioned off willy-nilly without a trace of planning or ecological foresight. Empty, undeveloped (but frozen from use) lots abound. One prominent California land use economist estimates there are enough empty lots in his state to support anticipated population growth for the next 100 to 300 years. It is of course not merely in California that lots lie empty for vacation or retirement homes; as early as 1966 the United States Census Bureau estimated some 12,250,000 lots lay bare—most of them unlikely ever to be used.

Most of those empty lots once were useful farm land, held in units of 200 to 300 acres. Yet the structure of America's agricultural markets combined with a taxation policy bordering on the belligerent to farmers without outside capital and

income, has made it all but impossible for small, labor-inten-
sive farmers to outlast the developers. The late Chet Huntley proved the lesson in exquisite grandeur when he fronted
for the Chrysler Corporation in Montana to build his Big Sky
recreation complex. From the day the first bulldozer blade
hit soil, the developers began crawling over the hills, tax
valuations shot up, and independent ranchers slowly began
to be pinched out of business. As each 200 to 500 acre farm
is subdivided, the markets, of course, become more concentrated, and the advantages have flowed increasingly to the
great corporate farmers. And gone are any quaint notions
that farming requires careful, personal husbanding of the soil
with a lifetime commitment to the land as the most vital
source of life itself.

The specter of corporate *latifundia*—for farming or fun—is
the future into which Wendell Berry and his fellow rebel
farmers in Kentucky do not wish to be dipped. To most
planners at the United States Department of Agriculture,
theirs is a position of ignorance and reaction, a horse and
buggy refusal to enter the twentieth century. To the extent
that the twentieth century represents a threat to the dispersed sources of democratic freedom, then Berry and his
band *are* steadfastly holding onto their buggies, even as the
French peasants have always held onto their artichokes
ready to roll them through the streets when bureaucratic
insanity grows too near. For Americans who have suffered
such submissions, the work of these Kentucky farmers is
both a solace and a call to revolt.

The fight for human control of the land is not limited
solely to those farmers threatened with dispossession. All
through it are woven strands of nostalgic, romantic mythology, near-primal remembrances of a local and national

life that seems much sweeter than today. It recalls a time of Norman Rockwell's ice cream and peaches paintings when students fervently believed textbook bromides about Jeffersonian democracy. But there is more. Land, and by it some variety of individual, family farming, recounts a symbolic history. What this nation has done to its land and to the people who have tended it is a story of loneliness, depression, and alienation following in the wake of great and concentrated corporate wealth. By now we have gone so far from the experience of living on the land that we have trouble articulating why that vision of life seems so attractive.

When hippies and cultural revolutionaries suddenly deserted the cities a few years ago on the crusade to build rural communes, they left, they said, because urban life was "a downer." A noisy, dirty fight just to stay alive. What they hoped to find, down in some green pasture, was relief from an urban brutality, be it high prices, dirty air, or street muggings. They also wanted a gentle pace, a chance to reflect on Thoreauvian delights. If their romantic scenario seemed doomed from the beginning, still it sheltered a pregnant irony. What city slave has not dreamt of getting away to the country, if for no other reason than because the city "is no place to bring up the kids." If only we could live "out there," it was said, we could be free, simply by the fact of moving out.

The idea was two dimensional. But it was no more so than the precious style of history most of us were taught, a history incapable of projecting profound struggles in human life. Nowhere in our Instamatic snapshots of the old farmhouse have we been asked to plumb the very special dialectic that binds together the life of the land and the lives of those who tend and nurture the land. Farming, like paintstore chemistry, was seen to be little more than following the directions on the side of the seed box: stir well and pray for rain. Rarely was it written that the ability to draw sustenance from the soil required years and years of hard learned husbandry, a keenness of touch, sensitivity and memory from which one knows—contrary to all scientifically ascertainable tests—that a certain corner of one field won't grow corn but it will grow grass. A propensity for mysticism is not required —among hip youth that has been all too easy a solution. Instead, it is more a healthy respect for how much is to be learned, of how complex is the physiology and the chemistry of the soil, about the earth and the limits to which it can be pushed. Nor do we find in our history much care given to the human business of working the land.

Work on the land *is* different. Most of the sociological jargon we use to explain the niggardly unhappiness of working life does not fit for land work. For those people who have either cooperatively or independently tended their own forests and orchards or tilled their own soil, work was never something apart from living. It was, and is, lonely and backbreaking. But until now landworkers were not divided from the products of their creation. Work was useful, intrinsically valuable for itself. Men and women who gave themselves to the work were capable of conceiving and understanding the whole enterprise. There were no assemblyline workers, blind to everything but a fragmentary job, fastening clips to hoses, day in and day out. The work was comprehensible and capable of being loved, if not always mastered.

It is easy to see the psychological toll on those who leave landwork for factory work. In Cincinnati, Dayton, Detroit, Indianapolis, all of them way stations on the great Southern migration from farm to factory, the mountaineers and the dirtfarmers are invariably the least manageable lineworkers and usually the last holdouts to industrial integration. Every weekend the highways south are clogged with mountain boys and their families "going back" until Sunday night, always dreaming that one day they might be able to return for good. Social planners and labor relations experts say these people are simply unable to change, that they are *culturally disadvantaged,* the marginal consequences of modernization. Why are they marginal failures? Because they have, eating away at their insides, a feeble optimism that says work need not be mean, pointless, and mindleveling, that the end of the day's work should bring tiredness and warmth instead of washed out resignation. There is a memory, submerged in us all, that our working lives can bring pleasure, even something so outlandish as physical and spiritual union, in fact that unity, that self integration can only come about through our collective attachment to a work whose completion enables and allows our own self-realization. The fragmentation and monotonous alienation of assemblyline drudgery is the antithesis of what work should be. That we all know. Only in our idealized notion of life on the land can we spot the fact that it once was different for all of us, that life and work were not at odds with each other. This then is the threat of industrializing the land, of manufacturing greater dividends for agribusiness, of running the cornfield by computer, not just that somebody is making a profit or that our food tastes worse and worse, but that a faint symbol of another variety of life is in danger. Furthermore, the threat is comprehensive.

In West Virginia, in Vermont, across the mountains and plains of Montana, down to Four Corners, New Mexico, and all over the Florida peninsula, the land rush has attacked every crevice of rural American life. Throughout the late

1960s and 1970s, financial analysts have shown how land investment has developed into one of the great modern business booms. Reflecting on the proliferating resort developments dotting the length of the Rocky Mountains, a recent former governor of New Mexico declared, "It is clear to me that unless something is done and done quickly, the Eastern Slope is going to become just another Southern California."

The first truly great corporate land speculators in America were the railroad tycoons. They fought viciously among themselves throughout the last half of the nineteenth century to gain control of the major transportation lines across the West. Control of transportation brought access to new trade and a direct hand in the actual administration of the new territories. But it brought more. As an incentive for the railroads to move west, the Congress provided free grants of public land along the rail routes. Some 130 *million* acres were given to the railroads between 1875 and 1900, over twenty-five times the total amount of land in New Jersey. Generally, the land came in a checkerboard pattern along the route line, railroad sections alternating with government land. The railroads were expected to dispose of the land within a very few years, either through sales to settlers for a few dollars per acre or through direct development. Instead, the railroads held on, often trading their land for other territories, so that in some areas they were able to consolidate hundreds and hundreds of acres on either side of the track and extending for great distances.

Today the railroads number among the most important farmers and landlords in the United States. Topping off the list is the Southern Pacific with 3.8 million acres; second is the Burlington Northern with 2.3 million acres, a hybrid combination of the Burlington, the Great Northern, and the

Northern Pacific railroads. None of the railroad land acquisitions is new. It is only the development of their lands that is recent. Burlington, for example, may soon become the undisputed master landlord of America. In early 1974 it announced plans to develop twenty-three sites in downtown and suburban areas on land that, for the most part, had been used as switching yards. Now those yards have become too valuable as real estate to occupy so much space for rail operations, and the switching yards have been transferred to the countryside. "We're packaging the land and we are experts at it," Burlington's chief real estate officer declared when the project was announced.[1] Hotels, high-rise office and apartment buildings, convention centers, and shopping centers will produce billions of dollars for these conglomerated railroaders on land that was given free for the common good, that was never supposed to be kept by the railroads in the first place.

When they don't develop real estate, the railroads are often leasing contiguous mineral rights, hiring out their land to large farmers (Southern Pacific leases its deep, rich croplands on the west side of the San Joaquin valley to Giffin, Inc., one of the nation's largest farms and for many years the second largest recipient of federal crop subsidy programs), or cutting away their vast timber holdings. Altogether private railroads hold over 20 million acres of land outright, nearly 1 percent of all the land in the United States.

Railroads are not alone. Timber and paper companies control even more land. A computation made in 1971 showed that the top twelve timber companies own about 35 million acres of land, almost twice as much as the railroads, or over 1 percent of the total. Companies like International Paper,

1. *The Washington Post,* March 2, 1974, p. E-1.

Weyerhauser, Georgia-Pacific, or Boise-Cascade have operations all over America, from the Pacific Northwest to the
southeastern coastal states to New England. "We have to
look at trees as a commodity, a property we need a return
on. We have that responsibility toward 55,000 stockholders," Boise-Cascade's chief forester said recently. But what
of the people who once lived on or still live adjacent to
Boise-Cascade's lands? By definition these massive holdings
are controlled by absentee landlords. Those 55,000 stockholders have no direct stake in what happens to local economies
and cultures where the land is located; if the soil is eroded by
clearcutting timber, the company's only responsibility is to
move on in order to assure that those dividends will keep
coming.

Nor is it merely the verdant blanket on top of the soil that
keeps the stockholders happy. Railroads, timber companies,
agribusiness outfits—all of them are keenly aware that the
real soul of industry resides beneath the surface: coal, oil,
copper, bauxite, uranium. Maybe more than anything else it
is the deep riches of the earth—in league with new housing
developments and the raw resources for food and shelter—
that have drawn corporate America to the land.

In 1972 the Appalachian Research and Defense Fund of
Charleston, West Virginia, compiled some data which might
show how West Virginia had fared at the hands of absentee
land barons. In a handful of the state's southernmost counties, where one-third of the population lives and from which
over two-thirds of the state's coal is produced, *nine* corporations own one-third of the land. Only one of them is West
Virginia controlled. The others include: Pocahontas Land
Corporation (a subsidiary of Norfolk and Western Railroad),
Georgia-Pacific, Western Pocahontas (a subsidiary of the

C & O Railroad), Island Creek Coal Company (a subsidiary of Occidental Petroleum), Union Carbide, Beaver Coal Corporation, Bethlehem Steel, and Berwind Corporation (a conglomerate holding company). According to a report written by the Fund's director, Paul Kaufman, in McDowell County (one of the three top producing coal counties in the United States), 76 percent of the land is owned by out-of-state corporations. The corporations who mine McDowell County and southern West Virginia are among the most profitable energy companies in the world. Since schools in West Virginia are 50 percent financed by local property taxes, Kaufman asked, wouldn't it be logical to assume that the McDowell Board of Education ought to be fighting for the kind of taxes which would support a good school system? In theory, yes. Except for the fact that the president of the board (in 1972) was a former United States Steel physician, another member was superintendent of United States Steel's operation for the county, and a third worked with a leading coal company. Furthermore, the president of the County Court (the county's administrative and fiscal body) is a member of a law firm representing Norfolk and Western, Island Creek, and several other coal or gas companies. The county's state representative is also a leading coal operator. So one-third of McDowell County's families make under $3,000 per year, the county's population has been slashed by half in the last twenty years, and not even half the county's adults have gone to high school. And the irony of it is that the companies claim great credit for the involvement their local officials take in "public affairs."

West Virginia is no different from other remote, rural sections of America where local control of the land and its riches have been taken over by outsiders who can regard it only as an exploitable commodity. In Montana, the Peabody Coal Company's chief local officer has publicly referred to the eastern third of the state as "one big ugly" that would be better off if it were strip mined. That, he feels, is ample justification for tearing up hundreds of thousands of acres of soil throughout the north central plains. Coal fields stretching from New Mexico to North Dakota are estimated to contain more than 2 trillion tons of coal and underlie 100 million acres. As the energy companies come in with their thirty-story digging machines, they promise to leave nothing behind but great mountains of upturned clay, poisonous streams, and dead farms. Citizens of the Rocky Mountain and northern Plains states have fought vigorously to prevent the strippers from moving in at full force. They have seen the results of four decades of stripping on such infamous places as Muhlenberg County, Kentucky, where the Peabody Coal Company, Pittsburgh & Midway Coal (Gulf Oil), and their lesser colleagues have virtually destroyed the area's traditional agricultural base. Peabody reported gross revenues in Muhlenberg County in 1971 of about $72 million. Its tax contribution came to less than 1 percent, or $188,848.49, proportionately less than the lowest paid janitor in the county courthouse. Many in the West have seen what has happened to this impoverished Kentucky county, and they realize that the threat is not simply romantic, not simply aesthetic, but in fact fundamentally material. Even if the stripping in Muhlenberg County were to stop tomorrow, it is doubtful the county could reconstruct an adequate agricultural economy to sustain itself. For the foreseeable future, its people are literally caged. They have no choice but to support the coal companies, for they know that when coal is gone, nothing will be left. They know, they smell, they see that their land has been taken from them, and that control over their own material destiny has been snatched from between their fingers.

One genial, hardworking, second-generation Scotsman recounts what has happened to the people and the land of Muhlenberg County. His story is aesthetic, but the aesthetics betray a bleak economic future.

"You take the road up to Rockport from Paradise—that's ten miles—and come over to Central City—that's ten miles —and then go ten miles down to Browder. That's a hundred square miles, of course all stripmined. There isn't anyone in there anymore. No one lives in a hundred square miles. That was solid farmland, and there was quite a bit of timber. Used to be you were hardly ever out of sight of a farmhouse, but no one lives there now.

"Paradise? There's just nothing there now—absolutely nothing. It makes me heartsick to go over there. A lot of people can grow older and go back home and say, 'Well, here's where I played as a boy.' I can't go back. There's not even any ground that I can walk over."

Small, private landowners are not the only ones to lose in the energy companies' land gobble. Most of the best mineral land in the West is federally owned and administered by the United States Forest Service, the Bureau of Land Management (BLM), and the Bureau of Indian Affairs. The conglomerate coal companies, most of which are now owned or controlled by international oil companies, such as Gulf, Continental, Occidental, Standard Oil, and the like, have not hesitated to move onto federal lands. A recent list of the ten largest coal leaseholders on BLM lands included Peabody Coal (Kennecott Copper), Atlantic Richfield, Pacific Gas and Electric, Consolidation (Continental Oil), and Kerr-

McGee. In June 1970 mountain state leases for mineral rights covered 58,905,110 acres of public lands. As one critic pointed out, that exceeds the combined acreage of New Jersey, New York, Rhode Island, Massachusetts, Vermont, Connecticut, and New Hampshire. The number has been booming since then. Finally, in order to mine and process the coal, millions of tons of water are required, and federal watershed projects have shown themselves only too willing to help. Energy specialist James Ridgeway has shown effectively how the Bureau of Reclamation has turned on the spigot to the coal companies in the northern Rockies and plains states. Of course, each gallon of water that goes toward huge coal operations is a gallon denied to the struggling farmers of the region whose crops barely get enough water as it is. And so once again local ownership and control of the land is squeezed out, with the help from the federal government.

2

Digging for Blue Chips

Everyone now knows that the family farm is dead. Population statistics have shown us all how the nation changed from a rural to an urban society about the turn of the century, of how 5 percent of the people produce 80 percent of the nation's food. Certainly, suburban homeowners realize how land prices have spiraled in the last twenty years. The story of land hustles, however, goes farther. Agribusiness and suburban lots are but one part. Knowing how to speculate in land, how to buy low and sell high, is a vast territory of special opportunity and creative development.

Land has become a reservoir for surplus cash. Insurance companies and conglomerates have put millions into land purchases and development all over the United States. Or as *Fortune*, the nation's leading business magazine, has noted, insurance companies may become "the largest landlords in America." Why insurance companies, or multi-national combines like ITT? There are many reasons, related both to the changing condition of the national economy and the particular needs of corporate planning and investment. Land has become a valuable asset for almost any large, stockholder company. A cross-section of the nation's biggest landowners will show international oilers like Mobil (Standard of New York), timber-based octopuses like Boise Cascade, the Southern Pacific Railroad, auto manufacturers like Chrysler Realty, Westinghouse electronics, insurance companies like CNA Financial or Aetna Life, or great mineral operators like Kennicott or Consolidated Coal. Each differs in its central reason for land investment. Timber and paper companies like Boise Cascade or Georgia-Pacific came to realize within the last decade that their vast forest holdings could earn much greater profits through diversified use. Coal companies have discovered that modest landscaping has both salutary public relations effect and potential recreational value. Choice railroad territory, acquired in the great land grant gifts of the nineteenth century, it turned out, was often high quality agricultural or ranch land. For the others, the new landowners, tax shelters and investment security available from buying relatively inexpensive land have proven very attractive in the overall strategy of building a conglomerate enterprise.

To the economic historian, these modern developments in land use and sales are not at all unusual. They are a natural consequence to private consolidation of basic resources, and if the physical and human landscape around us is becoming unrecognizable, it is only because we have failed to understand our own system of politics and economy.

Consider, for example, the case of Randall Sheffield, a small bean and cattle farmer in southwestern Kentucky. Sheffield owns 129 acres in Ohio County. With luck and good weather he just breaks even on the year's expenses. Still, he and his family like the life they've made, and they were even able to build a new house some years back and look forward to a modestly comfortable future. That was until the Peabody Coal Company visited his doorstep. Peabody Coal Company is the world's largest strip miner. It owns a big lump of Ohio County and over 50,000 acres of adjacent Muhlenburg County, made famous in John Prine's whiney ballad, "Paradise."

The Peabody Company does not want to take Sheffield's farm away from him straight-out. It just wants to drive a three-and-a-half mile coal conveyor belt across the farm and those of his three neighbors—blocking access from one field to the next, sending thousands of tons of coal roaring overhead each week, backing up drainage on the rich bottomland, and forcing him to drive beneath the belt to get to his home. The four farms are almost completely surrounded by Peabody's giant coal-stripping machines.

In most parts of rural America, a man's property is said to be his own to dispose. In Kentucky the courts say otherwise, citing as precedent a nineteenth-century statute that gives the mine operators the condemnation right to construct a "railroad, overhead conveyor, or pipeline" for transporting their materials to the "most convenient point" on a public railroad or waterway. So against his will, the Peabody coal train, stoked by the law, has ripped its way through Randall Sheffield's property.

Peabody's success, Sheffield says, will mean "the end of farming in the western part of Ohio County." The farmers spent nearly $5,000 in legal fees fighting Peabody, but through technical finesse on the part of the company, they were blocked from even getting to the state's Appeals Court. "I used to think that the law, through the courts, said something and that's the way it was," Sheffield recalled. "But you've just got to get that out of your head. They're there for the people that's got the money to pay for 'em." More than a little sorrowfully he explains: "You can't take a man to court that's got money. You can't do it. If you've got the money, you just don't have to worry."

"If these judges give 'em eminent-domain access through condemnation, how long's it gonna be before they want another little road over here, another one over there? It involves all these farms—they'll get 'em all eventually. In five years they'll have all the productive crop land in Ohio County sewed up. Most people—most businessmen, that is —don't see this. They just think that Peabody's going to bring in a lot of money and they'll get a little piece of it. They just don't grasp it.

"Who's going to pay the taxes? There aren't going to be any farmers to pay the taxes. You're not going to have people coming in here buying bacon and eggs and milk. Peabody'll just move on and strip somewhere else, up in Illinois or somewhere. There won't be nobody."

"Sell the country?" Chief Tecumseh is said to have asked. "Why not sell the air, the clouds, the great sea?" Randall Sheffield's complaint is much the same. When his land and that of his neighbors is reduced to the level of commodity, subject like a new car or a dishwasher for sale to the highest bidder, then the underlying structure of life in his community is foresaken. His complaint is at the nub of modern capitalism. Use value and exchange value are at the heart of the debate between socialist and capitalist economists, the latter arguing that it is the process of exchange, the trading of my surplus utility for yours to our mutual satisfaction which underwrites the free-market system. If an item's value is to be determined only according to how much it will bring in the exchange nexus, in the marketplace, the

simple consequence is that all other considerations—aesthetic, cultural, sentimental, whatever—must take a sec-
ondary role. The free-marketeer of course will respond that
the totality of values, social and personal, will be reflected in
the enterprese of exchange; if the personal and cultural sacri-
fices, subsumed under "externalities" usually, are too great,
then we will not exchange what we have, he would argue.
Postponing for the moment the problem of whether Randall
Sheffield or any of us live under a "free-market" system,
certainly our national ethnic subscribes to that view of social
affairs. It supposes that at the very least all objects are
salable and obtain their fundamental value from the price
they can fetch on the marketplace. The only anomaly here
lies in our quizzical and romantic view of land, of the sense
of security and social continuity that we invest in it. So we
are dismayed and angered when we see a decent man like
Mr. Sheffield surrounded and overcome because the pressures of trade have forced his neighbors to auction off the
physical foundations of their own homes and in the process
threaten his.

But what else might we expect, especially now that we
have seen how short are our fossil resources? At this instant,
for its present owners, Kentucky land is more valuable as
strip-mined coal than it is as beans and cattle. If the land is
to become another commodity on the market, then it is
hopelessly romantic to expect that it will not be treated as
such. That is the decision our European forebears made
some centuries ago with the birth of the enclosure movement
when it was determined that the earth was not simply the
common property of all its inhabitants but instead was to be
disposed privately according to the desires of the individuals
who controlled it. Privately held and owned, it was available

to be privately exchanged, like a role of silk or a twist of tobacco. Modern land speculation, be it by Peabody Coal or the Bank of America, is simply the current conclusion to our economic legacy.

We moderns have, however, developed some sophistication in our horse trading. It was largely through land that the nation's largest bank and its largest railroad achieved their current stature. And land takes no small role in extending the sovereignty of the world's largest and most famous international telephone company.

Banking, *Forbes* magazine once said, is the nation's fastest growing business. Bank of America, the nation's largest, is also one of the fastest growing banks. The complete story of BankAmerica Corporation's magnificent growth record is one of those quintessential California tales, replete with swashbuckling adventures, leathery-faced braceros along Salinas's Cannery Row, and a little gray haired Italian with a pushcart full of money. His name was A. P. Gianini. He founded and built the Bank of America, now a part of BankAmerica Corporation. Like almost everything else in California, Mr. Gianini's bank sprouted from the deep, rich earth of the state's central valley. The bank has never lost that legacy, and as recently as 1968, a retiring executive reiterated its special symbiosis with the land: "We are the world's largest agricultural lender with lines of credit for agricultural production running at about a billion dollars a year. Our total agricultural commitment is probably around $3 billion. We've been in agriculture for a long time and we intend to stay in agriculture for a lot longer. In a very real sense, then, agriculture is our business."[1] Just as California has become

1. Statement made by Randolph Paterson in a speech before the California Canners and Growers Association in San Francisco, 1968.

the symbol for "agribusiness," the Bank of America has been the preeminent "fixer" for the development of corporate agriculture.[2]

The Bank of America story begins during the Depression. While old Joe Kennedy was running booze in Boston, Mr. Gianini with his bank d'Italia (the name was changed later to Bank of America) was carting out loans to hard pressed farmers up and down the California Central Valley. The wiley Italian on the West Coast knew the same thing the old Irishman in New England did: even in the worst of times, some investments are failsafe, whiskey and land included. As the Depression grew darker and darker and the farms turned to dustbins, Mr. Gianini began to foreclose. Between 1926 and 1930, according to the Agribusiness Accountability Project, Bank of America foreclosed on over 1,300 farms. By 1936 the Bank's subsidiary, California Lands, operated 2,642 farms, producing some sixty crops at an annual profit of over half a million dollars. Land that was not sufficiently profitable was turned over to the United States government as a settlement on unpaid taxes. Those farmlands have never decreased in value, and although the Bank now only owns about 1500 acres outright, it holds tens of thousands of acres in trust, much of it operated or leased out to bank-appointed managers.

Today the Bank does not have to bother itself with the

2. BankAmerica's power, not only in California but also in the entire nation, only takes on full significance in the context of California's unparalleled position as the nation's truck garden. Not only is California the birthplace of agribusiness under Bank of America's auspices, it also supplies over a quarter of the nation's table foods, provides, about one-third of the nation's preprocessed fruits and vegetables, claims eight of the top ten U.S. agricultural counties according to farm products sold. Or as one West Coast utility company advertised, agribusiness offered investors a new Gold Rush: "Big crops—and a big variety of crops—make big business for farmers, processors, packagers, manufacturers and countless other industries. It's all Agribusiness—the number one industry in Gold Rush Country."

cumbersome details of small-farm foreclosures. In the first place it's hard to find small farms. More important, the bank has already accomplished the necessary capital transformation in restructuring the state's agriculture. It has become, for example, a prime advocate and beneficiary of the famed California Water Project, the scheme to divert the plentiful river waters of the north through and along the central valley by canal to dry southern California. That water was essential for irrigation which in turn insured the continued growth of massive fruit and vegetable farming, and hence the expansion of agribusiness (and the opportunity for lucrative investments therein) was directly dependent upon the success of the Water Project. Even more directly, the Bank of America was underwriter of the bond issue which payed for the project; and it holds some $600 million of the project's bonds. The Bank's former vice president for agribusiness, Robert Long, minced no words in explaining that the Water Project was valuable really only to the agribusiness operators, noting that "the water will not be available to medium and smaller operations." Users who could take advantage of the new irrigation, he emphasized, would have to be "a large-scale very well financed company."[3]

"Agribusiness is the biggest business in California, so the biggest bank should support it, shouldn't it?" Mr. A. W. Clausen, president of Bank of America once said. Yet when faced with responding to California's farmworkers, the bank seemed much less clear about its role. When, for example, it took over a 5,500 acre farm in the late 1960s through foreclosure, the United Farm Workers (UFWOC) tried to initiate negotiations with the bank. The bank wired the Farm Work-

3. Quoted by Richard Parker, "The Bank of America: An Annual Anti-Report, 1970," *Scanlans*, August 1970, p. 61.

ers that it had already leased the farm out to the Agribusiness Investment Company and therefore bore no responsibility. Conveniently, the four signatories for Agribusiness Investment Company happened to be two bank attorneys and two bank vice-presidents. And where was Agribusiness Investment Company located? After wandering over the hills of northern California, a nosy San Francisco reporter finally located the address: an empty lot in a small ramshackle town, with a nonexistent telephone number. Finally, one bank vice-president offered the following on the UFWOC grape pickers' demand for recognition: "We're not a dealer in grapes. The bank is not a farmer. It would be improper and unfair for us to take a position on this."

Small in its own right, Agribusiness Investment Company is nonetheless vital to understanding banks and land, especially the Bank of America. BankAmerica Corporation is a holding company for a variety of financial and investment institutions, including Bank of America which provides actual banking services. In 1973 ten of the sixteen board members of BankAmerica Corporation held directorial posts on important agribusiness firms, and several were the chief executive officers of large corporate farms. The character of the board, however, is only indicative of how the bank operates. Subsidiaries of BankAmerica Corporation like Agribusiness Investment Company are the key to its power and fortunes.

Legally, the banks are not allowed to muck about in manufacturing, marketing, and general business operations. Wisely, federal legislation was designed to keep banks out of direct domination of industrial and merchandising fields. Naturally, there is a loophole: the one-bank holding company. It allows the bank to walk right through the green mirror of financial reality and declare itself a "subsidiary" of a larger "holding company" or conglomerate corporation. As Bank of America's president explained in 1968: "A one-bank holding company presents possibilities for greater participation in a number of profitable activities, particularly overseas. While we have no specific business in mind, such activities might include leasing, warehousing, mutual funds, financing land development, travel bureaus, and other industries closely related to finance."[4] Come to think of it, what isn't related to finance, if you put it that way? So now, when the bank forecloses on farmers, it doesn't have to scurry about setting up dummy investment companies. Loan officers on the twenty-eighth floor need only ring up the trust and investment lawyers on the forty-fifth floor to work out the messy details. It's all so much neater, and the holding corporation can offer a much more rational profile on its land development operations once they are all consolidated in one place.

Through the holding-company concept, investment planners are able to see the land somewhat as Chief Tecumseh did. The land is no longer just pieces of a chaotic market: mining here, railroads there; suburban development on the right, farming on the left. Instead "land" takes on a new kind of integrity in which it is really an indivisible resource, a baseline which may take on any of a number of temporary uses. It is a rather perverse imagination that would warp the old chief's words so blithely, yet that is what operators like BankAmerica are doing. Newly acquired land does not take its value simply because it *was* a farm, but because it is a fundamental resource in the same financial category as all the corporation's other land holdings. How many of these holdings will be exploited depends not upon present or past uses, but upon what new or opening markets can offer.

4. Quoted in *The New York Times*, September 18, 1968.

A partial list of the 1972 BankAmerica acquisitions compiled by the Agribusiness Accountability Project illustrates how effective the corporation has been in using the holding company law to extend its land investments. Included are GAC Finance, BankAmerica Realty Investors, BA Mortgage Company of Denver, Envirotech Corporation, and Western American Financial Incorporated, all of which are concerned with land or real estate development and finance with assets totaling several hundreds of millions of dollars. Its record simply acting as a bank is similarly impressive. In 1971 alone it offered loans totaling $1.4 billion to California agriculture—some 40 percent of California's farm financing. Through its trust accounts Bank of America owns over 9 million shares of America's most profitable land and agribusiness companies. Among those corporations in which Bank of America holds at least 1 percent of the total shares are American Cyanamid (1.6); Amfac Incorporated (5.7), Pabst Brewing Company (2.4), Quaker Oats (1.8); Tenneco (1.0); and Union Carbide (1.0). In fact the bank's holdings are much greater, for in its own listings it does not include shares held by subsidiary corporations with "street" or front dummy names.

Testifying before Congress in 1972, A. V. Krebs of the Agribusiness Accountability Project stated the condition of California agriculture poignantly and accurately: "From its beginning—through a combination of massive land grabs, violence, foreign exploitation, political intrigue, slave labor, greed, the frequent ignoring of state and federal laws, and giant growing, processing, and packaging conglomerates (like the Del Monte Corp., Tenneco Inc., DiGiorgio Corp., and Sunkist Growers, Inc., with their interconnecting directorates) who control a vertically integrated flow of food from the field to the table—California's agribusiness has grown wealthier, more elite, and more powerful."[5]

"In its quest for total control of the state's economy," Krebs continued, "agribusiness has enjoyed the enriching benefits derived from state and federally subsidized water and transportation, abundant amounts of money from Bank of America, a free and unlimited use of the research facilities of land-grant University of California, and exorbitant United States Department of Agriculture cash give-aways totaling nearly one-half billion dollars in ASCS subsidy payments alone since 1966."

In 1969 6.1 of 11.8 million acres of cropland in California were owned by corporate farms. Bank of America's role in supporting that corporate take-over is absolutely crucial and very often directly instrumental. California, it has often been remarked, has led the nation for half a century in new cultural, political, and economic trends. Only since World War II have Americans realized how thoroughly ingrained are the nation's leading banks in dominating and directing its major businesses. In California the symbiotic relationship between the biggest bank and the biggest industry is even more tightly entwined. Moreover, it has heralded new economic trends for land ownership and development throughout the rest of America; it has helped open the door for many large or conglomerate corporations to enter into land speculation; and it has revolutionized economic thinking about how land is to be treated and used.

There is more to business than banking however. The

5. U.S., Congress, Senate, Committee on Labor and Public Welfare, Migratory Labor Subcommittee, *Agribusiness and Land in California: Hearings on Land Ownership, Use and Distribution,* 92nd Cong., 1st and 2d sess., 11 January 1972, pp. 730–41.

superstructure of American finance has created a second
variety of money company in the last quarter century—insurance. Except for banks, nobody has as much money as
insurance companies; in many ways they act just like banks,
extending loans for corporate expansion and opening up new
areas of development. No insurance is more deeply ingrained in the American consciousness than the rock of Gibraltar, hallmark of the Prudential Insurance Company of
America. Not only is Prudential one of America's oldest
insurance companies, it is also the richest, with assets of
over $29 billion. At the beginning of the decade it showed a
higher net investment income than any other large insurance company. As the company's own newsletter once
noted, Prudential's investments "in bonds, common stocks,
commercial and industrial loans, and real estate . . . are
seldom publicized, yet are mammoth in their size and complexity."[6] High on the complexity chart is land.

"We make real estate investments at the rate of roughly
$3.5 million on an average business day," a Prudential vice-
president noted in 1971.[7] Through its Property Investment
Separate Account (PRISA), Prudential managed at the end
of 1970 a portfolio of about $12 billion in mortgages and real
estate ownership with about 100 real estate offices. PRISA,
like a number of other Prudential subsidiaries, is also part of
a holding company called PRUCO, Incorporated. Prudential
Insurance Company owns all the stock in PRUCO, Inc.
while PRUCO, Incorporated, in turn, owns all the stock of
every Prudential subsidiary. Like BankAmerica Corporation, Prudential's holding company is a piece of financial
gimickry through which the insurance company can estab-

6. From Prudential Insurance Company's annual report, *Prudential People*,
Spring 1971, p. 6.
7. Ibid., p. 130.

lish a general management group to coordinate and arrange all its far flung investments.

Prudential is not modest about itself. Noting its well-known involvement in airlines, cattle ranching, and fashion, a recent company newsletter added: "beyond the investments we show on television lie thousands of other investments . . . in farms and factories, office buildings, hotels and motels, housing—the physical fabric of the United States and Canada that compromises the complex and constantly changing Prudential portfolio."[8] According to the Agribusiness Accountability Project, that portfolio includes an office building, a hotel complex in Houston, two farms equaling 5,000 acres in California where fruits, nuts, and field crops are raised, and securities holdings in some 712 land or agribusiness industries. As of January 1, 1970, those holdings had a total value of over $4 billion.

Speaking of Prudential's California farms, the company's vice-president for real estate investment has explained that in neither case is there "direct employment of labor. For the main part this is supplied by outside contracts." Certainly, farming on the rock of Gibraltar is an utterly different world from the sort of life Randall Sheffield leads in Kentucky. The tillers and sowers at Prudential do not even know the owners of the soil they work. They have no more reason to care for and nurture the land than assemblyline workers at General Motors have to make sure the brakes are properly attached. Nor does anyone there have reason to regard the land as a special resource to be regarded for its public value. It has no value inherent in itself other than its utility on the market. No one could state it better than the Prudential

8. From a letter from Prudential Vice-President J. E. Rutter to Agribusiness Accountability Project, December 9, 1970.

Company's own board of directors: "The composition of the investments held in the Investment Fund will be determined from the long-term view of a prudent investor concerned primarily with the preservation of his capital and the growth of his capital in relation to the growth of the economy and the changing value of one dollar."[9]

Randall Sheffield, of course, is concerned that he receive an adequate return on his money to give him a decent living. Whether he gets it, though, is mostly dependent on his skill as a farmer, on his ability to know and respect the soil for what it can and cannot do. His labor gives value to his product, and he is neither beholden nor responsible to absentee investors unknown and unseen. Furthermore, he knows that if he abuses the land, he will himself suffer disastrous consequences. For those faraway owners at Prudential who do not even know the men and women who work their land and whose only interest is that it return high profits—profits which may or may not be consonant with the long-run use of the land—there are no personal consequences for land abuse. Erosion, leaching of the soil, chemical poisoning may turn high short-term yields but may ruin the land for generations to come. For the diversified investment fund, that is someone else's problem, for then the land can be exploited in another manner or the investment shifted out of that particular piece of property. And then the land, like a used automobile, becomes scrap. Or, as a BankAmerica officer Lee Prussia replied in answer to a question about the ecological effects of the Bank's agribusiness policies: "A financial institution, historically and traditionally, has not been responsible for these kinds of decisions. We need not take a stand on issues of ecology."[10]

9. Prudential Insurance Company of America, *Annual Investment Portfolio Report*, 1969, p. 15.

10. Parker, "The Bank of America: An Annual Anti-Report," p

3

And Then There Were . . .

In 1973 the United States Department of Agriculture (USDA) issued a report detailing the use and ownership of farmland in America.[1] Soft-peddling the decline in the number of farms, the report noted that between 1971 and 1972 there had been only a 1 percent decline in the number of small farms, a figure which by its similarity to previous years would appear to be insignificant. Yet over the fifteen year period from which the data were drawn, 1959–1973, there was a 29 percent decline in the number of operating farms in America—a drop of nearly one-third. There were in 1959 approximately 4,105,000 farms in the United States; by 1973 that figure had dropped to 2,831,000. USDA farm acreage data sheds more light on the decline, for over the same period there had been only an 8 percent reduction in the land still used for farming. The reason is simple: more and more individual farmers were being closed out to big operators. Average farm size jumped by nearly one-third. Not since the Depression had farmers had such trouble holding onto their

1. U.S., Department of Agriculture, "Number of Farms and Land in Farms," USDA Statistical Reporting Service, Crop Reporting Board, SpSy 3(1–73), January 17, 1973.

independence as the big became bigger and the small grew closer and closer to extinction.

The USDA is very sensitive to discussions about the decline in small farms. The rise of anticorporatist populists has forced its economists and public relations specialists to be a little more guarded in their enthusiasm for bigness. For that reason official department publications almost always emphasize "the little guy." Citing new census data in 1973, the Department's Economic Research Service reiterated its argument that "corporations occupy a very small niche in the nation's farm economy." Farm corporations, it pointed out, totaled in 1969 only 21,513 or 1.2 percent of all farms in the United States.[2] Partnerships and sole proprietorships are easily the dominant farm types, accounting for 85 percent of all farms with sales topping $100,000. So, it is implied, even at the top of the sales ladder, it's the lonely entrepreneur who is most often in charge.

There are two problems with the USDA's proposition. First, "sole proprietorships" or "partnerships" do not necessarily indicate that a farm is personally or family run. Lyndon Johnson ran a family ranch, as does the famous King family of Texas; the great Byrd apple orchards—hundreds and hundreds of acres—in Virginia are also a family affair. Certainly no one familiar with modern farming would fail to recognize any of these operations as "agribusiness"; the legal nomenclature of their ownership is certainly more a matter of tax advantage than of any functional position in the economy. Even the USDA admits as much. "When it comes to paying taxes, a good many of our farm corporations are

2. U.S., Department of Agriculture, *The Farm Index,* vol. XII, no. 7, July 1973, p. 4.

treated as partnerships," a small sidebar to its corporate farming report revealed. Thus, almost one-third of the farm corporations filing tax returns in 1968 reported not as corporations but as limited partnerships. As long as the farm has no more than ten shareholders it is given this double option; each partner can then report his income individually thereby giving him the possibility of coming under the low capital-gains provisions. Most important for the USDA statisticians, it further muddies the already vague distinctions between partnerships and corporations. Thus, by concentrating on the legal character of ownership, the government analysis avoids a focus on the crucial issue for American farming: the continuing concentration of the whole farm economy into fewer and fewer hands.

Occasionally even the welter of government numbers gets to the point. A recent *Fact Book on U.S. Agriculture* suggested that hiring of farm labor might better indicate the real business character of a farm. It showed that 95 percent of all farms hire less than an average one and one-half man-years of labor (one and one-half full-time positions over a whole year). However, the same report continues, "The remaining 5 percent of the farms are also predominantly family-controlled businesses, but the operator and family members perform only a small part of the total labor required. These farms are much larger than family farms; *nearly two-fifths of the total value of all farm products sold in 1969 were produced on such farms*" (emphasis added).[3]

A few more figures make the picture even sharper, and they show the breakdown of farm income by sales category.

3. U.S., Department of Agriculture, *Fact Book of U. S. Agriculture,* no. 1063, March 1972, p. 20.

| ories of Farm Sales & Percentage of Farms & Net Farm Income, 1970 | | | | |
Value of Sales	Number of Farms	Percentage of Farms	Net Income	Percentage of Net Income
$40,000 and over	223,000	7.6	$25,664	36.4
$20,000–39,999	374,000	12.8	$ 9,962	23.7
$10,000–19,999	513,000	17.5	$ 6,208	20.3
0–9,999	1,534,000*	62.1[1]	$ 1,716[1]	19.6[1]

Source: Fact Book of U. S. Agriculture, p. 19.

1. Author's recomputation of lowest three categories: $1000–$2500; $2500–$4900; $5000–$9900.

Although there are relatively few very rich farms in the United States, the wealthy minority easily take the lion's share of all farm income. More than any other farm category the handful of wealthy farmers are able to exercise extraordinary control over the entire agricultural marketing system. Of course there are divisions by type of product that make it difficult to lump all farm sales together. However, the recent trend toward broad diversification in farm products, much like the scenario projected by the USDA, enables the large-scale operator to manage both livestock and field crops at the same time. A mere 7.6 percent of U.S. farms make almost twice as much money as 60 percent of the scattered independent farmers. Further reinforcing the privilege of the large operators is the disorganization and lack of cooperation by the smaller independents. The mere fact that 1.5 million small farmers, scattered all across the land, must carve up among themselves one-fifth of the national agricultural sales testifies to each one's weakness. Working on such near-starvation margins they are unable to have substantial influence on suppliers, transportation operators, or wholesale buyers. A few highly trained owner-managers dealing in huge volume (and largely in a half dozen big agribusiness states) are able to build their own supply and marketing systems and can achieve scale economies unavailable to independents and small-timers.

Peter J. Divizich is one man who knows about big farming first hand. Once he was a big farmer; his vineyard in Kern County, California covered 5,000 rolling acres. He also ran his own cold storage houses and packing sheds. And it all grew from just thirty acres of prunes he tended when he started there in 1915. His was family-style agribusiness, but in the hurdy-gurdy gardens of industrial farming, he still seemed to have straw sticking out his ears, especially after he was taken to lunch by the two great friends of California farming, the Bank of America and Tenneco, Incorporated.

Bank of America is an old hand at farming. For Tenneco it is a relatively new business, an entrepreneurial mutation for a firm established in the dark days of World War II to transmit natural gas by pipeline. Since 1943 Tenneco's accumulated assets have made it the sixteenth largest company in America. "We are told no other United States industrial corporation has grown this large, this fast!" the opening paragraph in its 1972 annual report proclaimed. As Peter J. Divizich found out, the Horatio Algers at Tenneco had distinctly more than prune juice and raisins on their minds.

Divizich spit out his tale in a choppy Yugoslavian accent before the Senate Subcommittee on Migratory Labor in 1972. The committee was chaired by Senator Adlai E. Stevenson of Illinois. With fifty years experience and 5000 acres to show for his skill, Divizich told how in 1965 he had hired the largest fruit and vegetable marketer in the country, Heggblade-Marguleas, Inc., to handle his grapes. That decision was the biggest mistake of his career. Sales tumbled, and although he dropped Heggblade-Marguleas after only a year, his losses were so severe that two years later he was desperate. The Bank of America was his principal creditor, and just as it had done all through the Depression years, the bank moved in to manage his farm. But his debt doubled, up to $9 million. In 1970 Heggblade-Marguleas and Tenneco concluded a merger. The bank finally foreclosed on Divizich and sold his farm to H-M, which on the side tipped another operator half a million dollars to withdraw its bid on the property.

Mr. Divizich felt he had received a less than delectable deal as he reflected on the fact that the company that had caused him the trouble ended up owning his land. So he sued Tenneco (H-M's new owner) and the Bank of America for mismanaging his property during the nadir of his financial dilemma. The jury agreed and awarded him $400,000 to be paid jointly by the bank and Tenneco.

If a grape grower with 5,000 acres and his own packing plant was unable to protect himself against industrial produce marketers, the ability of the real independent farmer who lives only off the soil has little hope of exercising any leverage at all. For Tenneco, a company whose gross revenues in 1971 were over $2.8 billion, a paltry $200,000 fine can get lost in the expense account chits. The comparison between the two operators is crucial.

Business reporters and agribusiness spokesmen have charged that the populist attacks on such companies as Tenneco —vertically integrated firms with operations in almost all phases of farming and food production, from fertilizers to tractors to supermarket display trays—are unfair. To some extent the apologists are right. Tenneco does not simply buy up the land, grow the seeds, spread the fertilizer, grow the crops, and then haul them with its own trucks to its own plants where they are packaged with its own plastic. Or at least it does not always do that. Instead, it does operate *laterally* through all of those levels in the industry. Through control of the nation's largest market, it is able to set the prices it will pay farmers for fruits and vegetables to be used in its packaging plants. With fewer and fewer marketers to choose from, the farmer has little choice but to take what the wholesaler wants to offer. The newest marketing scheme it has hatched is a gasoline-food store combination installed in Tennessee, New Jersey, Virginia, and Maryland. Tired of that long line waiting for gas? Then come inside for a six-pack and some tutti-frutti.

Getting Mr. Divizich's grapes was only practice for Tenneco's penetration into what it calls the "food and shelter" business. "In food," the company advertises, "we are marketing a premium brand of fruits, vegetables, dates and nuts under the name SUN GIANT in an effort to help independent farmers sell their produce while satisfying the high quality requirements of the consumer."[4] How helpful they were to Mr. Divizich remains open to some debate. "In shelter," the company continues, "you'll find Tenneco developing whole new communities with a commitment to total preplanning. Places for people to live and places to play as well as places to work and places to learn." Cradle to grave human packaging.

While its land operations are a small part of Tenneco's entire revenues (5 percent in 1971 and in 1972), they represent—as even *Fortune* magazine begrudgingly admitted—an almost classical model of corporate behavior.[5] Everything from the opulent Hyatt Regency Hotel in Houston to SUN

4. *Tenneco Annual Report*, 1972, p. 18.
5. Dan Cordtz, "Corporate Farming: A Rough Row to Hoe," *Fortune*, August 1972, pp. 135-39, 172-75.

GIANT fruits, nuts, and vegetables. SUN GIANT is Tenneco's effort to distribute expensive, premium quality fresh produce, and it is an international business, selling brussels sprouts in Poughkeepsie and oranges in the Orient. A new carrot packing plant in Southern California can handle 100 tons of carrots a day. Eighty percent of Tenneco's produce comes from independent growers, the company boasts, and it says in-house plantings are undertaken only to round out product lines and extend selling seasons. Perhaps. But that in no way diminishes its power over field agriculture, as demonstrated earlier. Quite the contrary in weather-perfect California, tightening up its control over marketing distribution is the easiest way to dictate production quotas and prices for even large-scale independents. Through development of long-term contracts with larger, corporate farms at least as big as Mr. Divizich's vineyard, Tenneco often can force the independents to conform to its marketing plans; having once solidified producer contracts, then any would-be mavericks who have their own ideas about farming are cut out of the market or forced to service only local independent grocers and warehouses.

As Tenneco's annual reports suggest, farming is only a part of what can be done with land regardless of what the original purpose may have been in purchasing it. Certainly, one of the great rural motifs of the last quarter century, widely reported in the business press, has been the steady conversion of farms to subdivisions, new towns, and home lots. Just a few of Tenneco's real estate developments in 1972 alone were: Columbia Lakes, a "pre-planned recreational-residential" subdivision south of Houston whose pre-opening and first year sales totaled $5.5 million; Pine Mountain Club, a second-home luxury play spa in the mountains above Los Angeles, the sales of which easily exceed $15 million; two twin nineteen-story office towers in Houston plus other smaller buildings there and rich property holdings around Houston and Brownsville, Texas, under the name of Palmetto Corporation, a wholly owned subsidiary of Tenneco Realty.

The rest of Tenneco derives its revenues from: shipbuilding ($462.3 million); automotive components ($178.8 million); construction and farm equipment ($609.8 million); pipelines ($699.8 million); oil ($657.6 million); packaging ($285.8 million); chemicals ($285.4 million); and general investments ($35.7 million).

Yet what does all this largeness mean to the consumer? It is easy enough to see that struggling marginal farmers are unable to compete with monoliths the size of Tenneco that always have enough cash to push their way around. But does it make any different to consumers where the groceries come from? There can be no doubt. In an essentially unregulated economy, diverse competition is the only condition that can give the consumer any control over prices. Dr. Paul Taylor, the distinguished economist now retired from the University of Califronia, explained some of the reasons to the same Senate committee that heard Peter Divizich's plight: "The decline in access of people to the land, a consequence of unabated farm enlargement and concentration of land ownership, is an important element in shaping the problems not only of farm workers but also of working farmers, town businessmen, and indeed all elements of rural society. The impact of uncontrolled, even assisted, displacement of smaller farmers by larger, even giant farmers is far more pervasive than simply obstructing farm workers and would-be farmers from the land. The impact is felt throughout the business, social, cultural and political life of the entire community."[6]

As a suggestion of the kind of contribution octopus agribusiness makes to its rural neighbors, we need only return momentarily to Tenneco Corporation. In 1970 Tenneco Corporation reported profits in excess of $73 million. How much income tax did it pay that year? Not one cent, according to its annual corporation filings submitted to the Securities and Exchange Commission.[7] In fact it picked up a handy $20 million credit. Even vice-presidential papers were never so good. For taxes, hardly anything is as good as oil and land, and Tenneco, of course, has both. Through pressing its oil depletion allowance, even as profits gush higher each year, conglomerate holding companies can write off untold sums made elsewhere in the corporation. Farming works much the same way, and agriculture is notorious for racking up paper losses (see Appendix A on tax loss farming). Small farmers who own only a few hundred acres and who depend upon the land alone for their livelihood get no such breaks. For them a loss is a loss, and they have no income from "manufacturing subsidiaries" to offset it.

Perhaps the most notorious advantages for conglomerate farmers come from the federal crop subsidy programs, known among many as the Agri-Welfare Roll. Farm-support programs grew out of the New Deal, a scheme to boost farm production through limiting the supply and thereby raising prices. The ostensible beneficiary was always supposed to be the lone dirt farmer who in a period of depressed prices could not earn enough to make his living. Somewhere it all

6. Senate, *Agribusiness and Land in California,* 92nd Cong., 1st and 2d sess., 11 January 1972, pp. 783–93.
7. Information cited in *United States Oil Week.* Reprinted in *Congressional Record, Hearing on S. 13524,* 17 August 1970.

may have worked according to plan, but since World War II, it is the massive farmers who have benefited the most. For example, investigative journalist James Ridgeway compiled data on the largest farm payment recipients in 1970.[8] Topping the list was the world's largest cotton grower, J. G. Boswell Company, a California farmer who controls almost 150,000 acres. Boswell's 1970 take was $4.4 million—not to grow cotton. Another big cotton subsidy winner in California was Giffen Incorporated, a 100,000-acre farmer who only took $4 million from the federal treasury. And third largest with $1.8 million in subsidy was South Lake Farms, a subsidiary of the Bangor Punta conglomerate, which among other things specializes in fire arms (Smith & Wesson), chemical mace, handcuffs, radar systems, and police-suspect indentification systems.

These are the people who get most out of killing off small farmers. What we get is high prices. It is from ranching and cattle raising that the consumer has felt the effects of big agriculture most. Meat, especially beef, has a special place in American dietary culture, or as a cattle raising subsidiary of L-T-V Industries put it recently: "Our meat is as American a necessity as red-blooded sports and red-white-and-blue bunting." Outside of small midwestern and southern towns, cattle raising little resembles the images most of us retain about bulls roaming through lush pastures. Formerly, beef cattle were grazed for one to two years before they were ready for slaughter. The kind of grass and corn they were fed determined the taste and tenderness of the roasts and steaks that eventually reached the dinner table. Now grazing hardly exists at all, replaced by chemical hormone stimulation that

8. James Ridgeway, "The Agri-Welfare Roll," *Ramparts,* September 1972, p. 10.

can enable cattle to be stuffed with up to twenty pounds of feed daily. The dangers of many hormones implanted in the steers (both for tenderizing and appetite stimulation) have caused great outcries but brought little response from the Federal Food and Drug Administration. Most of the fattening of commercial beef now takes place in such commercial feedlots, and their ownership is among the most concentrated of any element in the food industry. The 1969 Agricultural Census, for example, showed that *1 percent* of all U.S. feedlots handle over *half* of all beef sold while five companies buy 90 percent of all broiler chickens.

One of the biggest beef corporations, as described by writer James Rowen in *The Nation,* is Western Beef of Amarillo, Texas. Western Beef calls itself the "nation's second largest, publicly held, vertically integrated cattle company, with operations in Texas, New Mexico, and California." Western Beef buys its cattle through a subsidiary, then fattens, ships, slaughters, and reships the meat to supermarkets. Western Beef has not forgotten to read tax law either, and to take tax advantage has begun to manage so-called cattle partnerships. Rowen describes the loophole: "Any participant in a cattle partnership—investment is usually limited to high rollers in a 50 percent tax bracket—automatically may claim 'farmer' status for Internal Revenue purposes, thus qualifying for cash-basis bookkeeping whereby all expenses go out as business deductions, while profits return as capital gains."

And for those of us without "farmer status" who still like to eat beef, the results at the meat counter are all too clear. All the supposed streamlining that concentrated ownership should bring, cutting out two or three sets of middlemen who formerly had a piece of the beef business, has only doubled the price of hamburger. At the same time, grain costs for all farmers have as much as tripled in the last three years, so that the small rancher is swept along in the booms and squeezes created by the large operators. And how has business been for big beef? Western Beef's 1971 revenues, for example, were up over 30 percent from the previous year while its first quarter 1972 profits more than doubled first quarter 1971. *Fortune* 500 reports for 1971, 1972, and 1973 show that integrated beef operations are among the strongest companies on the list. In 1971 on the index of sales to invested capital, integrated beef concerns held five of the top ten positions.

Cattle, grain, fruit, fresh vegetables—the story of corporate agriculture repeats itself over and over. Each year the industry gets tighter and tighter, more and more resembling classic oligopoly. All the while food prices shoot nearly out of sight. For most of the last quarter century, the USDA has denigrated these changes, juggling its statistics to make it appear that corporations have an inconsequential role in modern farming. Yet having found that the data in their own publications belie their claims, the USDA has mounted a rising effort in recent years to wipe away the data altogether. How to do it? Easy. The most complete picture of American agriculture derives from the Agriculture Census, conducted every five years on the fourth and ninth years of the decade. The USDA itself does not conduct the census; that is the charge of the Department of Interior where all national censuses are conducted. However, the Census Bureau's arguments are direct reflections of the USDA's commitment to agribusiness. The Bureau's directors want to replicate Stalin's old trick of the 1930s where the ousted Trotsky was simply "erased" from official photographs; the Bureau's intention is to eliminate the Agricultural Census and integrate it into the general Economic Censuses. The Bureau itself admits that it conceives of itself as "agri-business rather than rural sociological in nature." The effect of its plans will certainly go far to define any farming but agri-business out of existence.

Not only has the Bureau argued for elimination of the Agricultural Census. In its 1973 plan to kill the '74 Census and integrate it with the '77 Economic Census, a schedule of minimum sales was proposed which would characterize an agricultural venture as a "farm." Unsure of the reception it might get, the Bureau offered three minimum cutoffs: $2,500, $5,000, and $10,000. Any farm making less than the cutoff simply would not be listed. As opponents to the proposal pointed out at the time, these redefinitions of farming would drastically reshape the statistical shape of American agriculture. At the $2,500 cutoff, 42 percent of America's farms would be eliminated; at $5,000 (the figure supported by the USDA), 56 percent would be eliminated; and at $10,000, 72 percent of our farms would be eliminated.

What difference does it make if the Census Bureau says America suddenly has half as many farms as the year before? There are many possibilities. If all the currently producing farms are eliminated for the satisfaction of government statisticians, why should the tax collectors not conclude these same farms are not really income producers and should therefore be regarded as hobbies? Or if the USDA is uninterested statistically in small farms, why should it continue to be interested in them for farm program benefits? Already the federal subsidy programs show a pronounced preference for mammoth operators. The ultimately consistent position is to eliminate the little fellows altogether.

Reporting in 1973 on the proposed change, *The Kiplinger Agricultural Letter* demonstrated plainly how much rosier the American farm picture would look if half the country's farms were dropped. "This change in terms would paint a new picture of agriculture. Farm numbers would be halved—from 2.8 million to 1.4 million. And net income per farm would skyrocket—from $5,500–$5,700 range to over $10,000, assuming no big changes in overall farm income picture. This would make farming appear more prosperous, since subsistence farmers would be dropped from averages. . . . An instant income boost such as this makes great political campaign talk."

Agriculture and Agribusiness. Our language is often disarmingly explicit in the brutality of its undertones. No linguistic specialty is required to sense the difference between the historic set of physical and human relations we mean by agriculture and the modern enterprise we describe as agribusiness. In the first is posited a manner of life and a dialectic condition. To do agriculture is what happens when man draws his labor to the soil, and out of it produces a means to survive. It supposes joint and reciprocal action among human beings, which overcame the isolated, individual pursuit of hunting and gathering. The emergence of agriculture was the point at which we established the trust of solidarity, a capacity to draw upon one another for our collective well-being, and therefore for something more than alien personal survival. Doubly dialectical, the discovery of agriculture was a discovery about the nature of self, of the realization that the insides of human pain and contentment were determined by our willingness and ability to lock arms with our fellows in order to live harmoniously with a physical terrain (nature) that will eventually overcome and absorb us. In the rise of agriculture, which was essentially the first humanist affirmation, we undertook at the same time the first ontological revolution. We attempted to come to terms with forces that had always spelled our destruction; in that revolution we began the building of interdependent culture and learned to create roles out of which might grow our own mutual happiness and delight. The history of agriculture, implied in the word's linguistic origins, is the story of humanist affirmation and deformation. Agribusiness is but the latest moment of deformation.

Agribusiness is the financial exploitation of land for profit through the techniques of industrial farming. The term itself denies all we would mean by culture; it implies no social pact, no need for human survival and happiness. It does imply alienation, that is, the breakdown of units in a productive enterprise and their separate, alien, utility. Agribusiness is understood to be neither more nor less than any other market investment opportunity; it is one way capital can be exploited to enlarge itself, and its managers assume that any human conditions which depend upon it possess instrumental value alone. Agribusiness is the best modern expression of exchange value as applied to the production of food. The dimensions of its cognitive power are therefore exactly limited. It is stark.

As is the prospect of its reality. Agribusiness is the mechanical future into which the United States government is leading us. Following is one description of how the United States Department of Agriculture has sketched out the ideal farm of the twenty-first century: "The wheat field is ten miles long. There is a machine—one colossal machine—harvesting the wheat, rumbling toward the setting sun on tracks which keep it from compacting the soil. A helicopter sprays pesticide on the adjacent soybean field. Another helicopter circles, scanning crop conditions, transmitting data to a computer. Two men sit in a bubble-topped control tower, watching the instrument panels which surround them. The lengthening shadows of three giant skyscrapers—skyscrapers filled with cattle—fall on the men. In these nearly fully-automated structures the cattle are fed various chemicals, fattened, killed, processed, and packed into cylinders for shipment by monorail to the cities. . . ."[9]

The vacuous aesthetics of the Agriculture Department's dream are inherent in the social promise itself. If the vision is harsh and offensive, reflective of what we imagine life to become after the holocaust, that is because the economic and social policy from which it is constructed represents the gears of centralized social destruction. Agribusiness is not simply aesthetically alienating; it is totalitarian, because for it to succeed as a viable planning model it must consume all of agricultural production, eliminating all other alternatives. There is no room for the independent farmer or for the cooperative farming community known to our grandparents. Agribusiness is the expression of a centralized, oligarchic control which demands thorough rationalization of the whole farming and marketing system, and finally of everything that we would eat and drink.

9. Larry Casalino, "This Land Is Their Land," *Ramparts Magazine,* June 1972, p. 31.

4

Buying a Place in the Sun

I had left Bozeman, Montana, just two weeks before Christmas 1971. Waiting for the train out—which had been stalled by a blizzard and 100-mile-per-hour winds up the track—I found myself filled with a melancholy anger. Five days I'd spent in this town of 18,000, nestled in the Gallatin River Valley of southwestern Montana, and it had been warm and friendly, with invitations to home-cooked dinners almost every night. Yet running beneath that sense of *bonhommie*, I had a gnawing apprehension that for the people of Bozeman this would be the last year they would share an ordinary, small-town Christmas, the sort where even the National Forest Service could welcome tree-hunters on public land without fear of abuse. By the next Christmas, it seemed, Bozeman would have ceased being the remote mountain spot of its last hundred years, for then there would be on its periphery one of the largest, poshest, most highly advertised resort "retreats" in the nation. Big Sky of Montana, Incorporated: chairman of the board, Chet Huntley; principal owner, The Chrysler Corporation of Detroit, Michigan.

Why Bozeman? There are several answers, each of them

shrouded in the dynamics of one of the largest land hustles modern America has experienced. The "recreational" complex at Big Sky is but one of a score of industrial real estate investments pocking the Rocky Mountains whereby giant national and international corporations are hoping to clean up on the annual escape of urban Americans to the wilderness.

Big Sky is named after the epithet first fashioned by novelist A. B. Guthrie. Guthrie was a Kentucky newspaperman who wandered west in pursuit of open air and rambling tales. He found both and wrote a best selling novel about the spirit of the endless horizon. For the last four years of his life, Chet Huntley made a business of Guthrie's imaginative tribute. Huntley was raised in Montana, and during the years immediately preceding his retirement from NBC news, he began to make plans to return there. His success derived from his local-boy heritage, which made him acceptable to the unflappable Montanans, and from his exact appraisal of how eager most urban Americans are to own a country place. Without a well-known homeboy like Huntley, Big Sky's backers probably could not have pried their way past local distrust of outsiders.

Just to be sure that Montana folk would remember him, Huntley ground out a tearjerker boyhood memoir titled *The Generous Years: Rembrances of a Frontier Boyhood.* It is a paean to the rugged values of range life, so sentimental that the reader expects Gene Autry to pop up out of the pages in a swirl of misty corral dust. Huntley opened the book with his first memory of Montana: "The iron tires of the spring wagon rolled silently along the twin wheel tracks worn into the grass: parallel trails wandering northward and away to their vanishing point on the treeless folds of the benchland. . . ."[1] From such a beginning the book rolls on like the swaying buffalo grass, an account of a free and open childhood calculated to make any grubby New Jerseyite's mouth water.

Big Sky, however, is anything but a rustic retreat. Blooming out of the Montana wilderness, it has been planned as a city of 100,000 people complete with smart shops, restaurants, ski and camping outfitters, a convention center, a host of service industries to maintain the "recreational park," overnight hotel accommodations for 1,000, 50 condominiums, over 200 private home lots, a sprawling trailer court, an 18-hole championship golf course designed with the help of Arnold Palmer Associates, three alpine ski runs, plus tennis, swimming, snowmobiling, canoeing, archery, fishing, skeet shooting, and horseback riding—"all just moments away." It is touted as a place where people "live the good life all year around." One brochure proclaims, "A Big Sky mountain home is in partnership with nature and the leisurely pace of western living affords the perfect retreat from the pressures of business and position."

Such a partnership with nature must undoubtedly make the herds of deer and elk feel like very junior partners. Just as junior are the people who happen to live up the road at Bozeman, who have watched stoically as the Big Sky Master Plan quietly reconstructed their town in its image, and many of whom believe that Big Sky has turned into a public swindle to the profit of the railroads and the impoverishment of the public.

The birth of Big Sky was announced in January 1970, two years after the appearance of Chet Huntley's book—and

1. Chet Huntley, *The Generous Years: Remembrances of a Frontier Boyhood* (New York: Random House, 1968), p. 1.

four years after Huntley began discussing the project. Struck by the fondness the TV hero seemed to feel for his first home and led by the Chamber of Commerce, Montanans at first welcomed Huntley and the new jobs he promised to bring with him. Since resistance to speculative intruders has always been strong there, even Huntley admitted Big Sky probably could not have made it through the door without his name at the top. Now, when it seems almost too late, a growing number of Gallatin Countians would be just as happy if he and his generous plans had stayed in New York —or at least away from Bozeman, Montana.

Though they have not succeeded in stopping Big Sky, these Montanans have effectively raised several core issues surrounding the acquisition of public lands by absentee corporations and the environmental impact of turning the Rocky Mountain wilderness into a playground for the wealthy. They also stung the late Mr. Huntley to the quick, causing him to drop his well-modulated demeanor and shoot from the hip at his opponents. Just a "band of extremists," "30-day ecologists," he called them, mimicking the Agnew-style epithets he had deplored previously. Yet in the first two years of fighting, over 1,000 local citizens signed petitions protesting Big Sky's plans. The "band of extremists" leading the attack have included nationally prominent members of the Forest Service and State Department of Fish and Game, engineers and geologists who work at Montana State University, and a major environmental research firm in Denver.

Joined together as the National Forest Preservation Group (NFPG), they have concentrated their opposition not against Big Sky per se, but rather against policies of the National Forest Service that have allowed public lands to be released for private development. As always in the West when land is the issue, the great railroad lines have been involved intimately. Only 100 years ago all the lands in southern Montana were Indian territory, most presumably guaranteed to the Sioux, Cheyenne, Shoshoni, and Arapaho by treaty. The Northern Pacific Railroad, along with several legions of U.S. Cavalry and some mining prospectors, had something else in mind. The Northern Pacific, determined to blow open a gateway to the Pacific Northwest, and hence to commerce with the Orient, elected to build a railroad through Montana, along the Bozeman Trail that had been so valiantly defended by the Sioux and the Cheyenne.

Despite twenty years of struggle, time and technology yielded success to the white man, and the U.S. government made good on its grant of 33 million acres to the Northern Pacific using its checkerboard maneuver. Sometimes, as in this instance, previous settlers' claims alongside the tracks forced the government to offer lands farther than 100 miles from the tracks. This ownership pattern, reasoned the government, would enhance the value of the publicly held land as private owners initiated urban and agricultural development. Recently, the large landholders have begun to realize the potential of the vast tracts of wilderness and first quality timber that could be theirs for a little simple trading. The Northern Pacific (now the Burlington Northern) consummated its first exchange several years ago for the stated purpose of developing well-managed tree farms. As NFPG Coordinator Russel Berg explains, there was little opposition to that exchange since the use patterns and environmental dimension of the affected lands would not be changed. Now the Burlington wants to effect two more exchanges, but the object is somewhat different.

Throughout 1971 Berg's group appealed to the Forest Service hierarchy for a reversal of a local decision approving the railroad's Exchanges 2 and 3, until eventually the decision lay with the new secretary of agriculture, Earl Butz. NPFG's two principal objections were that the appraisal and valuation of lands involved in the exchanges favor the Burlington Northern and that the potential recreational uses of the traded lands violate laws governing disposition of public lands. When they were appraised in 1968, the public lands in Exchange 2 were assessed at $8.02 per acre and the private lands at $12.48. By 1970 a reappraisal had set them at $25 and $51 respectively, a three-fold increase of the selected public lands and a four-fold increase in the offered private lands.

An exploration of such evidence might seem to be a needless exercise in isolated detail especially since the acreage prices remain low. The catch is that laws governing land exchanges require rough equity in value between lands exchanged and lands received. Burlington Northern has made much of the fact that if the exchanges go through, the public will receive almost twice as much land as it's giving. Nice deal? "Well, it might seem like it," Frank Culver, a geology graduate student and NFPG member, explained. "But you have to understand what kind of land we, the public, are getting." He pointed off to a range of snowcapped peaks called the Hialite Range. "A lot of what we're getting are the tops of those mountains which are so steep you couldn't do anything with them anyway, and most of the rest is within Yellowstone Park about 80 miles away." By Forest Service estimation, 62 percent of the lands going to the public are described as rough and steep, while none of the public lands to be taken by the railroad are so described.

Berg and Culver also question the revised appraisals themselves. They argue that the private lands are without any potential for development to justify the increased valuation. Conversely the $25 per acre assigned the public lands (some 1,920 acres of which the railroad will immediately sell to Big Sky) is vastly underrated—based as it was on the price Big Sky paid for its land *before* the development was announced. Land prices throughout the county have since shot up, and since Big Sky was the first purchaser with recreational intent, their price in fact came at a bargain—well below what newcomers can expect once the resort is open.

Since 1970 some of the public lands—about 5,000 of the 10,000 acres the Burlington Northern will receive in the exchange of lands—have been further revalued up to $90 per acre. Yet by the mid-1970s land prices had already exceeded $1,000 per acre, promising rapidly to hit $2,000. "It's a $10 million swindle," Russel Berg declared. At $90 per acre, the railroad had only to pay through exchange the equivalent of $500,000, while the prices everyone else was paying were approaching ten and twenty times that much. At market value—a market value largely established by Burlington Northern and Big Sky's activity—the railroad would have had to provide land worth between $5 and $10 million.

The logic is not completely lost on the Forest Service. Checking out ski developments in Colorado, its officers came up with acreage prices running from just over $150 to near $1,000. However, they restricted the comparability of those prices to areas immediately adjacent to the Big Sky Mountain Village, ignoring both current market trends and the fact that all the lands going to the railroad are close to Big Sky and have topography suitable for development.

These appeals and arguments are not new. But aside from minor concessions the Forest Service response has been, in effect, "You're entitled to your opinions, but this is what we're going to do." Candidly, regional foresters in Bozeman admit that the laws, regulations, and policies of the Forest Service are designed to encourage productive agricultural and recreational development—as the Walt Disney flack over Mineral King in California demonstrated. Montanans like Frank Culver and Russel Berg agree that the roots of their fight embody fundamental issues of social and economic policy. How and for whom will the few remaining, unblemished lands in America exist?

"We're not against putting up a ski run up there, and maybe even something like Big Sky would be a good thing. But the open lands are a vital resource to this country, and we're against giving away any public lands at all. If they were moving a whole community of people out of some Eastern ghetto, giving them new homes and really redistributing the population, then it would be different, but these are going to be second homes for the wealthy. Instead of opening up the land, it's going to mean that more land will be cut off from the people."

No outside "preservationist," Culver is a tall, lean Montanan with just a fleck of mountain brogue in his voice. At thirty, he's already picked up two degrees in business administration. Four years ago he began to notice what was starting to happen to the great open expanses of Rocky Mountain landscape where he'd hunted and hiked as a boy, and he figured he couldn't just sit around while it was all laid waste. So he went back to school at Montana State, where he has a graduate fellowship in the Earth Sciences Department and later became secretary of the NFPG.

Since Frank Culver began to watch the changing landscape more carefully, he has seen the land crunch grow tighter and tighter. From Glacier Park near the Canadian border to Mexico the cash registers in real estate offices are clattering like slot machines. Montana's *Great Falls Tribune* stated the situation succinctly: "Montana is for sale in the classified sections of national magazines." In Madison County, where most of Big Sky's holdings are located, family holdings have been turned inside out. Two decades ago some sixty families owned ranches in the county's Ennis Valley; today 80 percent of the valley is held by a half dozen owners from Illinois, Indiana, California, New York, and Wisconsin. At Virginia City, the county seat, a company quaintly identified as Montana's Treasured Land Corporation bought 1,281 lots at $15 each; by 1972 about 100 had been sold for $350 each, *sans* waterlines and sewers. Western Montana seems to be carrying the brunt of the new developments.

Colorado is not the only endangered state. More sparsely populated than its Rocky Mountain neighbors, Montana may become an even juicier target. Big Sky, for example, is just one of four major corporations which have nearly surrounded the mostly public Spanish Peaks Primitive Area. The other three are: the King Ranch of Texas, Fred Combs' Diamond J Ranch, and the Irvine Company's Flying D Ranch. Irvine, the largest landowner in California's Orange County, deserves special attention. Six years ago Bill Fairhurst, an active sportsman and subsequent mayor of Three Forks, Montana, was driving along the Madison River on Bear Trap Road as he had done for some twenty years whenever he went hunting for deer and elk. He came up to a gate as usual (for this was a "prescriptive-right" road, a road on private land which, because it had been used by the public for over seven years, was classified as publicly accessible). But this time, something was different. "There was a 'no trespass' sign nailed to a post, and the gate was padlocked. Just beyond it a small tent was pitched, and what came next was a real surprise;

"A man carrying a 30/30 stepped out of a tent and walked toward me with the gun pointed at my belly.

" 'I want to go through,' I told him, nodding toward the gate. 'Will you unlock it, please?'

" 'You're not going through,' was the surly reply. 'I'm working for Flying D, and I'm here to keep people out.' "

Flying D had by closing off even county roads (now reopened) tried to block access to 100 square miles of publicly owned lands east of the River. Bill Fairhurst, also a birthright Montanan, talks bluntly about what the corporations are doing: "They're turning public land into a private club for their board of directors and a few personal friends." Speaking in tones of populist radicalism, he lays blame right at the corporate door step, and he doesn't hesitate to add that he came to his understanding directly from having to fight the facile lawyers and hired guns of organizations like the Irvine Company. He concedes that Big Sky and Irvine are winning the land fights. "They can spend all their time fighting through the courts. That's their job. They've got the capital to do it. But people like me don't have the time and the money. They've got other jobs."

What of Big Sky itself, that rustic partnership with nature where each condominium (starting price $27,000) has its own garbage disposal unit? As Chet Huntley explained, capital is the name of the game. Capital like: Burlington Northern, Northwest Orient Airlines, Montana Power Company, Continental Oil, The Meridian Investing and Development Corporation of Coral Gables, Florida, the General Electric

Pension Fund—and most important of all, with 52 percent ownership, the Chrysler Realty Corporation, a wholly owned subsidiary of Chrysler. Always number three in the car business, Chrysler started dealing in land in the early 1960s when it was buying up property for company dealerships. By 1967 land seemed to be doing as well as cars, and Chrysler Realty was formed; at the end of June 1970 assets exceeded $416 million, generating pretax earnings of $7.7 million.

Chrysler also owns one square block of Manhattan, a new town called Northfield Hills just north of Detroit, a block of condominiums in Honolulu, a Chicago Loop office building, a student living complex at the University of California, Riverside, plus commercial and residential properties at Las Vegas, Ft. Lauderdale, and Boca Raton, Florida. Chet Huntley and his colleagues have declared adamantly to their neighbors that Big Sky is not a real estate development, that it is simply a "recreational area." Chrysler Realty's view differs somewhat. Specifically describing a series of projects including Big Sky, Chrysler president Edwin N. Homer says plainly, "We are also moving into general profitable and promising corporate diversification."

Another of Frank Culver's co-workers, Michael Gonsior, is keen to the distinction. Big Sky has drawn up a color-coded master plan and an environmental study statement designed to govern the resort's growth. Gonsior, who was recently appointed to a major Forest Service study team, finds liitle comfort in it. "They had a beautiful master plan down at Vail [Colorado] too, but it didn't take any time to toss it aside once the investors decided they weren't getting out what they had put in. The way Big Sky is set up, it can do the same thing." Big Sky officers boast that they will develop no more than 25 percent of their holdings, and that a set of "protective covenants" prohibit property owners on the development to violate the general plan. There is a small catch though. The owners of 75 percent of the property are permitted to abandon the restrictive covenants should they so decide, which means that Big Sky itself has the power immediately to abolish the tight environmental controls property owners are guaranteed when they buy in.

Since its inception, Chet Huntley has made much of Big Sky's environmental approach to development. To be sure, Big Sky's developers have taken several unusual steps. A tertiary sewage and water treatment recycling system has been installed—the only one of its kind in Montana. Special effort has been taken to prevent soil erosion on the ski slopes, and there have been several predevelopment surveys to determine wildlife concentration and surface water purity. Plans call for solid waste to be deposited in landfills.

Yet the tone and choice of issues in Big Sky's Environmental Report seem more an exercise in preventive reaction than ecological construction. Both that report and the Forest Service's Environmental Impact Study were submitted to the Rocky Mountain Center on Environment (RMCOE), a nonprofit environmental consulting agency in Denver. RMCOE's evaluation acknowledged that Big Sky had done more environmental planning than most other land developments in the country, but in general it found both studies grossly superficial. Offering praise for preliminary tests and surveys undertaken, RMCOE pointed out that "it was not clear . . . how all this data is being reviewed and coordinated into a meaningful and useful ecological statement about the areas proposed for development." For example, while Big Sky declared that its land "is not a part of any migration route" and is not a winter range, it offered no substantiating data. More important, Big Sky has not owned the land long enough to chart wildlife grazing patterns. Conveniently omitted is any mention of the adjacent Spanish Peaks Primitive Area where several species of wild animals roam. Big Sky studies have included only those areas to be developed, excluding such contiguous areas. Writes RMCOE, "It does not make ecological sense to limit the wildlife study just to Big Sky itself. Relationships must also be drawn in terms of surrounding wildlife communities." The same can be said for the development of a 27-hole golf course (in a habitat only averaging thirty frost-free days per year), the construction of a paved road through Big Sky lands, or the soil composition and drainage available on land that is to receive solid waste. Of course there are an infinite number of problems which might be examined, and Big Sky's environmental critics do not ask for their exhaustion. Rather the problem is an absence of coherence, the absence of an ecological context which would account for the interrelated effects of any important change in land usage—especially in a locale where the life blanket is as fragile as it is on Big Sky's cold, rugged terrain.

Perhaps the costs would be prohibitive for planning on such a scale. Big Sky is projected to cost nearly $20 million, by completion, and as sales of condominiums rise and fall, many people wonder if the company can make it on its own master plan. Sea Ranch in California and Snowmass-at-Aspen both dropped well-balanced plans as soon as it became necessary to recoup some "front end" money. Chet Huntley once stated the problem himself: "We cannot expect the private sector to pay taxes on land and simultaneously reserve it as a public park or wilderness area or recreation facility." Huntley at the time was arguing that the proposed land exchanges would give the public ownership of those high wild lands owned by the Burlington Northern. The only guarantees that such areas "will serve the public interest for perpetuity is public title to them."

Nonetheless, Chet Huntley was a nice man who really wanted to save his state. Of course so do the people who live there all year and who never had the resources to jet back and forth to New York. ("Oh, I guess I've been back four or five times last year, so you might say I have the best of both worlds," Huntley once remarked in a personal interview in December 1971.) He liked the small town values, the fact that nobody needed to lock his front door. Even so, he was convinced things had stagnated in Montana and that more people were needed to stimulate business. "Well, we can't build a fence around Montana," he used to say, while Big Sky President Gus Raum remarks, "If people want to come here, I'm sorry but I can't do anything about that." When pressed, Huntley and his colleagues would admit that Big Sky could do better with a few more people in Bozeman —say about 100,000, "that'd be about the right size." That would also constitute a population explosion of over 500 percent.

Chances are Big Sky will get its needed people. "It just doesn't make any sense," Huntley explained, "90 percent of the population on 7 percent of the land." How could Big Sky effect that redistribution? It helps to have friends, good friends like Senate majority leader Mike Mansfield and the Department of Transportation. Huntley and Mansfield had been buddies for more than twenty years, and in the two years of appeals over the public land transfer, they kept a regular correspondence. Should the Forest Service consider reversing its decision on the appeals, Mansfield has left no doubt that he would be unhappy. In a letter to the chief of the Forest Service one year ago, Mansfield made it clear he found the appeals process a mere formality and urged the Service to expedite its work as soon as the appeals period was exhausted. Two months later Mansfield wrote the Chief Forester again, enclosing a letter from Huntley, stating his own support for Big Sky, and adding, "Quite frankly, if we cannot bring about developments of this nature, I do not know ,in what direction the state can turn and at the same time provide the necessary input to keep the state financially sound. Those few who protest have not to my knowledge offered any alternatives." Mansfield's letter was marked "Personal" and scrawled across the bottom was an extra note: "Chief, This is most important to Montana & its development. M.M."

A few months later Big Sky inherited another windfall when the Department of Transportation designated it an "Economic Growth Center," thereby enabling it to receive federal highway construction funds to improve access to the development. "Completion of this development alone," stated the Montana Highway Commission, "will mean a considerable boost for the economy of a number of southwestern Montana counties, and the further developments it will undoubtedly stimulate will have more far-reaching effects . . . . The high priority assigned to this project results from the simple fact that if the needed transportation facility is not provided, then private capital committed to the area will be withdrawn." The maximum population a growth area may have to qualify for funds is 100,000.

To the Bozeman Chamber of Commerce or the Gallatin County realty board, a city of 100,000 would seem the ros-

iest possible future for southwest Montana. Most Montanans, however, are members of neither organization. They are
ranchers or farmers or employees of a few scattered service
industries. They are not a transient population, and outsiders
are welcomed only if they are interested in contributing to
community life, not if they are interested in temporary speculation. But Montanans are caught these days, caught in a
system of agriculture that supports only the large farmers
well. Even if they should try to expand their farms or
ranches, they have little chance of success because the recreational speculation has driven prices up so far that production cannot support the higher acreage prices.

Recreation may be the only alternative left now. Some are
already lining up with Chet, suggesting that the entire state
should be developed in projects much like Big Sky. If they
have their way, Montana would become a giant sprawling
park, its body bared to those affluent enough to escape for
a month of leisure each year to their own private hideaways
in the most beautiful and rugged corners of the widerness.
Already the people of Gallatin County have been given an
idea of what to expect. A recent study on local air traffic
reported fewer than 50,000 passengers arrived or departed
from Gallatin Field in 1971. Normal projected growth would
have increased air traffic to 126,000 by 1980. When traffic
related to Big Sky was included, the projections jumped to
300,000 by 1980 and 425,000 by 1985. Direct New York and
Chicago flights will be added, jumbo jets will operate in and
out of the airport, and the area now available for parking will
be taken by a single car rental agency. Who among the
residents in this bustling city of 100,000 will be able to go
camping or hiking remains a tough question. The Forest
Service has already eliminated most of its free or nearly free

campsites, and the public land left may well be barricaded behind the massive game preserves of large holding companies.

Handing over federal forests in Montana to the railroads only hints at how much money is to be made on America's compulsion toward rural escape. Maybe even more harrowing is the widely told story of how the Forest Service in California brought in the dazzling Walt Disney operation to turn the fragile mountain terrain of the Sierra Nevada into a $35 million recreation extravaganza that would entertain over 12,000 visitors daily. In Florida the situation is even more precarious, for the delicate balance that has long existed between water and land is being ruthlessly upset. The same financial greed that has ripped apart the verdant blanket of Florida now threatens the fragile screen of life across Montana and the Rocky Mountains.

Florida, in fact, is perhaps the most total tragedy in the history of American geography. Every schoolchild remembers the wondrous tales Spanish explorers, who first landed there in the sixteenth century, told back in Europe. Overwhelmed by its lush beauty, they immediately named it *Pascua Florida,* Feast of Flowers. By the mid-1970s, the combination had left even the Everglades burning. In April 1974 as I drove north from Miami, the heavy, sour smoke of burning forests drifted across the highway—and April is still within the rainy season. That most of Florida has been up for sale for the past two decades is almost a cliché. Until 1955 Ft. Lauderdale was a pleasant village by the sea, crisscrossed by winding residential canals. Today high-rise condominiums block out any view of the sea and are distinguishable from New York's Upper East Side only by the pastel color of their walls. Club swinging cops and sun-baked coeds are further evidence of the almost total transformation that has taken place here.

Yet the high-rise decline of Ft. Lauderdale is only the best known story of Florida development. Billboards along Highway I–95, the main north-south corridor into Florida, advertise new residential and investment developments in almost every quarter of the state, from the nationally known Mackle Brothers to the newest scheme in preplanned living by International Telephone and Telegraph (ITT).

ITT is the future, its billboards promise. And the future is called Palm Coast, a product of ITT Community Development Corporation located between St. Augustine and Daytona Beach. The case of Palm Coast does not resemble public land scandals like Big Sky or Mineral King. It does not involve public lands, and there is no way the previous owners of the land can claim a roguish swindle by their successors. And while some owners of ITT-built houses at Palm Coast may complain of shoddy construction, there seem to be no outlandish malefactions. Palm Coast is simply the best and most carefully sold development in North America. The issues it raises are more simple: Is this the sort of futuristic city in which Americans would like to live? Is this the way Americans want their lands to be used?

Palm Coasters live by the sea, or at least within a mile or two of it. Through the middle of their development runs the Intercoastal Waterway, a canal system which runs from Miami to New Jersey and can accommodate ocean going ships. ITT brought its Florida lands for about $10 million; in 1974 it claimed sales of over $200 million. Today only 300 families live at Palm Coast, but within ten to fifteen years, ITT promises there will be a city of over 700,000, and that city will use up more land than either Detroit or Philadelphia. There are many more than 300 owners of land at Palm Coast—the developers will not say how many—people who have bought lots because they believe the sign they read as they walk through the front door of Palm Coast's Welcome Center: "Tomorrow belongs to those who act today. Before the year 2000 this land will probably be gone because Florida is growing faster than any major state. . . . More people mean less land and real estate property values have soared 78 percent since 1964."

If the first sign is too subtle, the road-weary driver from the industrial north only need twist his head slightly to the right. There, in liquid color, is an eight-foot photograph of a coastal sunset, and below it: "This is the land, lush, virgin, promising. When fully developed it will probably have greater dollar value than all the gold shipped past these shores by the Spanish kings. . . . You can have a place in the sun . . . it's here now—Palm Coast—a better place, a better way, a better life."

Beyond the Welcome Center are the model homes, slapped together with very thin timber but attractive. Because this is a middle- and working-class development, and not one of the retirement estates for the elderly rich, every fixture in the model houses is cemented down: the plastic bananas and the antique, painted polyethylene telephone, the dirty coffee cup in the steel sink, and the book *Seven Days in May* in the bookholder, opened to the morning of the marine invasion.

Above the Welcome Center, in the heart of Palm Coast, is a control tower, with windows on all sides, where every square foot can be watched or examined or displayed with a proper telescope. From the control tower stretch out the bulldozed acreage—all the way out to the treeline where ITT harvests pine forests planted in the 1930s, 1940s, and 1950s. Pine timber makes good cheap building material. Once the forests are cleared, the development moves further out. At first, Palm Coast called itself another Venice because its canals lace the property; now the canal building project has been stopped by environmentalists who complained that no provisions were made to keep the canals from stagnating and filling up with algae. From the control tower one also sees Palm Coast's highly publicized "tree-saving program." On most new lots there are no trees left. Company officials explain that tree saving—palms, cypresses, and live oaks some varieties of which take centuries to mature—really means tree transplanting.

Like the transplanted palms lining the driveway up to the ITT Sheraton hotel across the main canal, they are twenty and thirty feet tall and dying. As I toured the property, I asked the young woman driving our courtesy bus if the trees had been blighted by spring frost. "Oh no," she said. "They're dead, or at least dying."

"Why?" I asked. "Have they been here long?"

"Only a few weeks," she answered as we passed a massive garbage pit filled with television packing boxes. "They cut off too many roots when they planted the trees. They cut the roots off to the same size as the leaves. That didn't leave enough, I guess. It didn't work."

"Will they replant more trees?"

"Oh, I suppose so. Maybe next time they will live."

Back across the main canal by boat, we hopped into another courtesy bus, driven by Doug. Doug is a Vietnam veteran who, naturally, prefers not to talk about his days as a foot soldier around bloody An Loc. He doesn't live in Palm Coast, but he has bought "a piece of land here," and in his spare time he wanders over to the club (which he notes is decorated in modestly colonial "African Coastal" motif) and muses about how he sure wouldn't be working here if he had as much money as the people who run yachts up and down through the main canal.

As Doug hops back into the bus, he reminds the would-be Palm Coasters, that "Palm Coast is a preplanned community. Anything that happens, or might happen here, we're ready for it. Every eventuality has been planned for."

"You mean there're no surprises if you live at Palm Coast?" I joke.

"Well, there's not supposed to be," he answers quietly, driving on.

Just before we get to Dr. Norman Young Parkway (Dr. Norman Young is president of ITT's Community Development subsidiary), Doug stops the truck. He nods across my lap to a gray, cement, windowless building on our right. "That's the phone company's control system. Once we have enough people here, that will control the most advanced phone system in the country. Every house will be linked up so you can control everything in the house from outside, dial your number plus a special code number and you can have all your calls rerouted for the evening, or with another code, you can call up from the beach and start the oven cooking dinner all by itself." Doug lets out on the clutch, and we start to move again, nearing the end of the tour. We turn around in the driveway of an empty lot and pause again. "See that white building over there. Well, it's not really a building. It's a replica of a river paddle-wheeler. We thought," he smiles at us all beguilingly but in earnest, "we thought that'd fit in real well with our concept of a water community. And, and that heavily crowded area over there behind it will eventually be an island, and there won't be any building on it. Uh, yeah, right now it's just sort of a peninsula formed by the canals, but then we'll cut the other side off. Something for the people."

Not all of Dr. Norman Young Parkway is complete yet, but that, the Palm Coast guides eagerly explain, is a sign that Palm Coast is a young community. When it reaches maturity Palm Coast will be completely encircled by the Dr. Norman Young Parkway. Dr. Young occasionally drops in at Palm Coast, Doug explains sometime during the tour, but it's not very often, because, you see, Dr. Young is a very busy man, attending board meetings and making speeches all over America. It is no wonder he is in such demand; Dr. Young is very unusual, and he does have a vision of tomorrow. Among other things, Dr. Young is a former dance-hall bouncer and New York ad man. He also holds a Ph.D. in psychology.

"The solution to the problems of a city," he once told a reporter, "is to have someone enlightened own it and control it." He blinks at the thought that anyone should consider ITT less than enlightened. And certainly ITT will control everything at Palm Coast. *The Nation* once called Palm Coast not just a development, not just a company town, but a "company city." ITT will, for example, provide its own water and sewer service, managed by another ITT subsidiary, Atlantis Development Corporation; of course, it has its own timber that is mainly controlled by ITT Rayonier, a smelly pulp plant 100 miles north; and it provides its own armed ITT-Pinkerton police who drive around in company owned patrol cars. Most important, ITT has claimed the right to tax property owners. It claims that right because most of Palm Coast's land requires drainage, and a 1913 state law gives the principal landowners in an area the right to tax their propertied neighbors for any desired drainage works. The two biggest landowners in the district are ITT Community Development and ITT Rayonier plus subsidiaries of both; together they have formed the Atlantis Water Management District; the "Management District" would have the power to tax for drainage programs, thereby giving the company the power to decide what to drain, how to drain it, and how much taxation is required to carry it out.

Drainage, Palm Coast agents insist, really isn't a problem though; the land is high, they say. President Norman Young, responding to conservationists who worry about alligator-infested Graham Swamp being surrounded by Palm Coast, explained it once like this: "We have no swampland. We just have areas of high elevation where there's trapped water that needs drainage."[2]

An investigative reporter for the *Miami Herald* once visited Dr. Young to learn more about Palm Coast than is described in the single, one-page flyer available at the Welcome Center. Confronted with the notion that some people have doubts about Palm Coast's vision of tomorrow, Dr. Young unleashed his tongue with characteristic swagger: "A lot of people are challenging us and criticizing us, but if we and our kind of people get hit and stopped, this country is going to be in even worse shape than before. People are trying to blame the country's big developers for screwing up the cities, but this country wasn't ruined by developers. Builders built this country and the average builder puts up less than fifty houses a year. They're the ones who ruined our cities, because they didn't have the resources to do it right!"[3]

Neither is Dr. Young afraid to talk about the kind of world

2. Michael Toner, "ITT Subdivides Paradise," *The Nation*, May 1, 1972, p. 564.
3. *Ibid.*

he is building. It is all in his statement of welcome, paint-engraved on a large panel just inside the door of the Palm Coast Welcome Center. If the language seems garbled, even unsyntactical, it nonetheless possesses all the catch-phrase hopes and fears of a troubled urban America.

"We are proud . . . because here we will have what is best for man in his environment . . . abundant recreation for the full leisure life; ample and easily accessible roadways for freedom of movement; the extension of purity and life of our air and our water and because the only containment within this community will be those placed on all polluted elements. Here at Palm Coast we will have a community of vibrant involvement; not one of vegetative existence, but of participation in all that makes life exciting. Physical activity will be coupled with stimulation of the spirit and time for all the good things.

"You are part of the greatest land development in the world, but we do not want to impress you with its size, but fulfill you with its promise, stimulate you with its content, and nurture you with its clean air, pure water, soothing sounds, and aesthetic beauty.

"We all want to live the good life, the life of contentment and to fulfill this desire we must see to it that the country we live in has planned for tomorrow while dealing with today, anticipate the problems of future generations while serving needs and dreams of the current populace.

"Welcome. . . ."

Palm Coast is one kind of "new town" development, the sort whose entrepreneurs have taken empty, wild scrub land and filled it up with housing tracts. None of the others has been quite so heavily promoted as Palm Coast, with its sales agents scattered around the globe. So far none of the others has seemed quite so big. But Palm Coast's is a standard technique: buy the land cheap, bulldoze in a few improvements, and then sell off lots to inflation-ridden Northerners anxious to make a buck on the land boom. Registrations at the United States Department of Housing and Urban Development (HUD) record millions of such operations, albeit most of them on a more modest scale, all across western and southern rural America. Beyond doubt, Palm Coast is better than the inaccessible desert plots or submerged swamplands offered by many notorious land hustlers in recent years. (The nation's largest operator, General Acceptance Corporation, was ordered in spring 1974 to repay $19 million to customers who had been sold such worthless "retirement investments.")

Yet for grandeur and simple audacity there is one land "developer" in a class all its own. It is the biggest private land holding in America, and it is among the oldest. It has been one of the biggest agribusiness operators in the United States, boasting at one point the "largest bean field in the world." It provided the land for one of America's richest seaside resorts and is the only major development to win a tour and endorsement from President Nixon's domestic cabinet. It claims the nation's fastest growing industrial park and it will soon have four freeways crossing its midriff. It pushed through a nationally noted state law to protect farmers from being taxed as developers and then used that "reform" to avoid taxes on its own future developments. And its internal history is a *tour de force* of death, destruction, and corporate intrigue.

Its name is the Irvine Company, and of course it is in California.

5

The Private Planning
of Paradise

Ray Watson was pressed but dutiful. Within a quarter hour he had promised his daughter he would leave the office in time to make her high school graduation over at Eastbluff. Now there were two journalists plopped into the red round upholstered lounge chairs at the front end of his office. We (my researcher, a mostly retired student agitator from Berkeley and Stanford, and I) had come, insistently, into his life to find out what he was doing as president of the largest planned city-company in America, the Irvine Company of Orange County, California.

Our questions seemed perfunctory. All we had to do was look out either glass wall of his seventh-floor office. To the west and through the corner was the blue Pacific Ocean. Closer still, a ring of ultraelegant houses protected by secu-wealthy surf and sail community and the second one of California's most important underworld drug markets. Closer still, a ring of ultra-elegant houses protected by security gates and built on landfill along the mouth of Newport Bay. Immediately below us was Newport Center: a shopping mall called Fashion Island, enclosed by an oval drive and staked into position by five high-rise towers, one of which housed Watson's office.

We turned as Watson pointed through the north wall. Another ring of exclusively planned "villages," one of them perched around the perimeter of a captive country club. An airport, second busiest in the United States with an executive jet parking lot the size of two football fields. Beyond it, the Irvine Industrial Complex, fastest growing in the United States. Two north-south freeways. A few more high-rent villages. Then green fields and orchards from which premium asparagus is flown daily to Paris and tree-ripened oranges are trucked across the continent. And behind the green fields, at the foot of the mountain, are four corrugated steel sheds where the Mexican bracero workers live. Irvine is a planned community.

Throughout the year and a half I'd spent as a magazine editor in California, gothic mythology had continuously seeped up from the Irvine ranch and its luxurious surroundings, as though the whole complex—its ubiquitous freeways, the tireless surfboard set, the utter absence of anything resembling a "downtown," and the never ending feuds of the Irvine family—were some private Hollywood incubator for the bizarre. The very starkness of the University of California campus there had lured MGM's horror moviemakers to film *Beneath the Planet of the Apes* somewhere between the Social Science and the Chemistry classroom buildings.

Always close to the desert crust of suspicion and paranoia were footnotes dropped by the Irvine Company apparatus itself. Old cases like that of Myford Irvine, last male heir to head the company, found tucked up in the corner of his basement in 1959, two large shotgun blasts in his belly and a

.22 bullet through his head. Suicide, ruled the coroner, and the basement was subsequently destroyed by fire. Or James Irvine II, lovingly known as J. I., found floating face down in a creek on the company's Montana ranch while on a fishing trip in 1947; seems he had had a furious row with a junior colleague the night before, but a week after the funeral the same colleague convinced the board of directors the old man had promised him a company loan of $190,000. Or of milder but more recent vintage, a team of Catholic service workers teaching English to bracero farmworkers, run off the ranch at dusk by one of the company's armed deputies.

Eager to keep all these details in order, I had asked an old friend to send a packet of company history so I could study up before arriving, but alas, the company had failed to include all the footnotes. It did include, however, a handsome almost-parchment-like map of "Historical Sites on the Irvine Ranch—Northern Half." Each site is marked by an appropriate symbol, guns for shootouts and nooses for lynchings; of the former I discovered there had been four worth noting, and three of the latter. That of course covered only the mountainous northern half; how the statistics added up on the more active southern coastal plain was left to the imagination.

My map of past gore, plus the newspaper accounts of more recent events, were scant preparation for the clean, cool style of modern warfare in the corporate womb: a fifteen-year battle by a beautiful, blonde family heiress to wrest control of the company back into family hands (i.e., her hands) and away from a cabal of outside lawyers, accountants, and businessmen who took power subsequent to her grandfather's death in 1947, the same outsiders who convinced the old man to put his ranch in the hands of a James Irvine Foundation that they, in turn, controlled. Though he was a new arrival, company president Ray Watson was clearly on the outsiders' team.

As we sat behind the polarized windows of Ray Watson's office, these were, of course, details left quietly beneath the surface. Ray Watson is a planner, a city builder, a man who talks of urbs and exurbs, of the inners and outers of metropolitan living, and of the impossibility of standing in the way of growth. He is part of the new team, the men who are waving goodbye to the ranch's agricultural past and who hunch over real drawing boards turning out the newest thing in city planning since Venice dug canals: long, rolling fairways called "Greenbelts," the key to happy living in the city of the future. Greenbelts will return graciousness to urban living, and if there is anything Watson finds important about the Irvine Company, it is its trailblazing record in building Greenbelts. But more about Greenbelts later.

Whether it was the newest gimmick in city building or the latest formula for fresh frozen cactus nectar, Ray Watson's dazzling lifetime opportunity derives from finding himself in charge of the largest and most valuable piece of private property in California—83,000 acres, or one-fifth of Orange County. Irvine owns another 11,000 acres in California's Imperial Valley and an extra 100,000 in Montana. From his boyhood in an Oakland rooming house, it is a dream that even he must find unlikely, to be head at forty-seven of a company that is building a city six times the size of Manhattan.

Such American success stories do not bring tears to the eyes of the blonde heiress, forty-one-year-old Joan Irvine Smith. To her, architect-president Ray Watson and his college-trained managers have been nothing but obstacles. As second largest shareholder in the Irvine Company (she has 21 percent; the Foundation has 54 percent), she has shown herself willing to leap continents and push through an act of Congress to dissolve majority control held by the James Irvine Foundation, whose votes hired Watson. If she is ultimately successful, she stands a chance of becoming the richest and most powerful businesswoman in the world. Right now her Irvine stocks alone have been estimated as high as $200 million. To take control and expand her wealth even further she must displace Watson and the Foundation management he represents. But first some background on how she and Ray Watson reached the shooting gallery.

Don José Sepulveda headed just one of a dozen old Spanish families who struggled to hold on to their boundless land grants when California came into the Union in 1846. These great land barons had dominated every facet of life up until that point, but as the years passed so did their wealth and grandeur. Slowly, they began to sell off their land—rolling windswept ranches of 20,000, 30,000, 100,000 acres—as speculators and traders pushed down from San Francisco and Los Angeles. Some like Sepulveda were driven to the roulette wheels and the crap tables and from there to the land hucksters. One such was an Irish immigrant from Belfast named James Irvine. James, aided by two partners, founded the Irvine dynasty when he unloaded Sepulveda and two other decaying families of some 110,000 acres, over one-third of it purchased for the magnificent price of fifteen cents an acre.

James Irvine soon pushed his other two partners out, and when the Southern Pacific Railroad tried to drive its tracks south through his land, he rounded up an armed posse for a midnight showdown. He did not, however, believe he had built an ancestral estate and, except for a tense miscarriage of his last will and testament, the whole ranch would have been sold at public auction. In fact an auction was held on July 16, 1887. Two strong bidders emerged and as the auctioneer closed bids, a dispute arose over who had made the final offer. Advised by the court that the entire sale could be canceled, family heir J. I. Irvine, Joan Irvine Smith's grandfather, pulled the ranch off the market and preserved for another century a landscape that would blossom with intrigue.

The night sky on most summer evenings at Irvine is a quiet contest. A soft blue haze piles up on the eastern mountains until it spills over and extinguishes the smog-filled blaze of an ocean summer sunset. There is none of the balm that bathes a sweet Carolina evening. Chill fog blows in from the sea. Earth is barren, but for suburban trees imported by the city builders.

I wanted to know how it felt to breathe and touch and smell this new American city. So, first night, I went down to the Newporter Inn, the very spot where two years before Martha Mitchell was attacked by five guards armed with a drug-filled hypodermic needle, the same Newporter Inn whose seasoned manager "died" from "a fall in the kitchen" a month after Martha's attack, the same Newporter Inn whose rear terraces display green floodlit pools in the shape of pigs' kidneys and whose front door spits out flaming Hawaiian luau torches a few feet away from an authentic imitation French bistro called the Café de la Paix.

From my café table I followed the summer brown line of Irvine hills almost to the offices of Nixon lawyer Herbert

Kalmbach, two floors beneath the office of Irvine president Ray Watson. A choice spot to reflect on the Irvine "heritage" described by another recent company president: "For over 100 years, members of the Irvine family and company have tended this land. We have raised cattle and sheep here, planted crops here, built our homes here. Now, as other families arrive to make the old ranch their home, we must communicate the respect and love we feel for the land. We must work to keep this century-old heritage alive."

That is the heritage old J. I. Irvine (James II) left. However, like his father, he finally showed waning interest in reserving that heritage for his family. At his heyday he had used the ranch for farming: 25,000 acres of beans were planted during World War I (the largest lima bean field in America), and there is still about that much land reserved for farming. Only a few thousand acres, which now mostly form the beach cities, had been sold for development. Confronted with the mid-Depression death of his elder son and namesake, plus growing urban pressure and exploding corporation taxes, he took the advice of his accountant and vested controlling interest in the newly formed James Irvine Foundation.

Joan Irvine Smith remembers well the nights she sat on her grandaddy J. I.'s knee. He was her favorite, and she his. As she grew into her teens and the hints of striking beauty began to appear, J. I. even brought her along for horseback rides or business lunches. Friends who have known both Irvines say she is just like her grandfather in temperament and ambition. Her father died when she was only three, and in that rare relationship with her grandfather she learned early on that certain people—herself included—have a heritage worth preserving, an option on the future.

She did not wait long to exercise that option. As Ray Watson, the architect-planner from upstate Stockton, worked his way up through the company, Joan Smith merely laid out her 21 percent stock interest and took a seat on the board of directors. That was 1957 and she was twenty-four. Not for a moment since then has she ceased her campaign to destroy the James Irvine Foundation that has controlled the company and its land development since her grandfather's death. Hardly a year has passed when she has not used her one-fifth interest in the company to block some management plan.

Her prime enemy, though, has been Foundation chief N. Loyall McLaren, the accountant who first persuaded grandfather Irvine to set up the Foundation. He became president of the company after Joan's uncle, Myford Irvine, was found dead in the basement, officially a suicide but allegedly a victim of Las Vegas mobsters who expected him to put $5 million into land now underlying Caesar's Palace. McLaren, now in his eighties, plays Pygmalion for the whole show, Joan alleges. Titular company heads like Ray Watson she has labeled "puppets." She spares no ammunition on McLaren and his associates. Speaking at the University of California's Irvine campus in 1971, she practically accused him of criminal conspiracy:

> The pattern here is clear. How often has history repeated itself. An ill and aging gentleman [her grandfather], bereaved by the loss of eldest son [her father], is manipulated by a clever and ambitious advisor; the old gentleman, who is convinced after much persuasion, that through the creation of a Foundation, he can preserve his life's work in perpetuity—in essence, will rule his kingdom from the grave. What follows then, but the unnatural deaths of both the old gentleman and his only remaining son [her uncle]. The last adult male heir is not even cold in his

grave before the clever and ambitious advisor takes over. He has waited a long time to control this empire, and he has laid his plans well. With only women and children left now, the path is clear.[1]

With like candor she went on to describe McLaren's "ruthless tactics" and his ability to rule with the "strong-arm methods of a dictator."

"However," she warned, "his feudal baronage is fast nearing its end."

The difference between a feudal baronage and a rich heritage, I soon discovered, depends upon who wants to wear the crown. I drove up the freeway the next morning to L. A. where I was to see Joan Smith's chief gladiator, attorney Lyndol Young. I had called ahead at nine o'clock to be sure he would keep our noon appointment. Young was past seventy, and I feared his schedule might be somewhat erratic.

"Hell, boy, I been here since 6:30 A.M. Where you? 'Course I'll be here. Breakin' a lunch appointment just to see you!"

For eight years Young has done nothing but fight for Joan Smith's cause. He zips back and forth across the country almost as often as the presidential jet, checks into the Watergate when he is in Washington or drives on out to the Smiths' Middleburg, Virginia horse estate about an hour away. Except for her, he says he would have retired years ago. He is loud and rambling in his speech, this big blustery man with age in the face. I began simply enough: how did he and Joan Smith want company management to change?

"Change?" he railed. We don't want to change 'em. We want to get rid of management altogether!" Young's account

1. From Joan Irvine Smith's speech before the Association of Students of the University of California Irvine, Irvine, California, December 7, 1971.

exploded with a Byzantine order of character attacks and criminal innuendo. "Our basic challenge has been the mismanagement of the Irvine Company by the Foundation and its trustees who have 54 percent control over it. The beneficiaries of the Irvine Company have been defrauded of millions of dollars in dividends"—which, he assured me, was a violation of federal law regulating foundations.

Relishing his own courtly rage, Lyndol Young proceeded to explain that all this went back to Joan Smith's grandfather, J. I. "McLaren (J. I.'s accountant, now head of the Foundation) convinced him half the ranch would have to be sold when he died just to pay the taxes. Then McLaren told him this Foundation was the only way to beat the taxes." Young paused and added, "The old man hated taxes more than anything."

The problem now, Young explained, was that stockholders like his client Mrs. Smith weren't getting anything out of the company—a paltry eighteen cent dividend when he began to represent her in 1966. And though her one-fifth ownership of the company was enough to block many projects, she could not force management to pay her higher dividends.

"So we went to Court," Young said. There he tried a new tactic, arguing that the entire people of California were being cheated by a tax-dodging foundation that was paying its company officers fat salaries while paying out a pittance each year to charity, its technical function. The judge apparently liked Young's argument but told him there were no legal precedents to rule in favor of his client: "He told us Congress was the only one who could do anything."

So Mrs. Smith went to Washington. She and Young roamed the halls of Congress, visited the Treasury Department (then considering foundation legislation), and even-

tually teamed up with antifoundation crusader Wright Pat-
man and tax czar Wilbur Mills. For three years they testified
before congressional committees, lobbied, lectured, made
friends, and presented their case. Finally, the 1969 Tax Reform Act produced just the law Joan Smith and Lyndol
Young were looking for. Where the courts and boardroom
fights were unsuccessful, Congress had produced results.

Not only did the new legislation require the Irvine Foundation to dump its stock, leaving Joan in majority control, a
clause had been written into the federal law—applicable
really only to Irvine—which would force the foundation out
of the company faster than usual, within ten years. Other
foundations were given fifteen years to dump any majority
stockholdings. But then Joan didn't want to be an old woman
by the time she took over.

Lyndol Young boasted proudly about that particular
clause. "I pushed it in!" he exclaimed, nearly shouting. "I
knew what a damned bad actor the Irvine Foundation was,
and the Committee knew what a bad actor it was too!"

Young didn't stop there. He went on to explain what a
ruse and a fraud it was for a charitable foundation to control
hundreds of millions of dollars but not be required to spend
them on charity. Irvine, he said, had hardly spent $1 million
a year, and there it was worth $500 million. Young, the
Congress, and a good many business analysts have claimed
the Irvine Company is worth $1 billion, and the Foundation
owns half.

Wouldn't I agree, he demanded, that a charitable foundation ought to be giving to charity? It did seem reasonable, I
conceded. Well of course, he continued, and that's why the
tax reform law required foundations to start giving more
money to charity, between 4 and 6 percent of their assets

each year. Those requirements just happen to give the Irvine Foundation a big pinch, forcing it to give away from two to five times as much to charity as it ever had before. And where could the Foundation get that money? "Well that's just the point," Young declared. "Either they're going to have to tell the company to pay the stockholders more dividends, or they're going to have to sell their stock to raise the money."

In either case, he beamed, Joan wins. If dividends go up then she, like all the stockholders, gets more money. If the Foundation has to sell its stock to raise money, then she gets control of the company even quicker. Already the strategy has paid off handsomely in increased dividends. "In 1966," Young said, "Mrs. Smith was paid eighteen cents a share; yesterday, at the board meeting, through blood, sweat, and tears I got that up to sixty-nine cents a share; that means in 1966 her dividends paid her $275,000, and this year, 1974, they'll pay her $1,040,000. That's right, each one of those increases was done with blood, sweat, and tears," he repeated.

All of which has taken the case back to Washington where Joan Smith and Lyndol Young found the law they needed. There the Internal Revenue Service (IRS) is trying to figure out just how much Irvine is really worth. If Young's figure of $1 billion is right, then the Foundation will be forced to spend as much as $20 million a year for charity. Irvine's own assessor said the company was worth only $189 million.

That, said the IRS, was ridiculous. Property taxes alone would suggest the company was worth $500 million. So the IRS decided to make its own assessment, the final determination of which should tell Joan Irvine Smith how long she must wait to take over.

For years, students, professors, and rankled citizens had railed against the Irvine Company, condemning in the most vitriolic terms the way it had "bought up" local government in Orange County. Nothing, they said, be it zoning, taxation, or building a public park, could be undertaken without the express approval of the Irvine Company and the Foundation executives who ruled it. Yet no charge against the company could equal Lyndol Young's admission that using Congress had been a major part of Joan's struggle for control of the company.

"Part of my strategy?" he had barked. "That was all my strategy! I took this to Congress in 1966. My whole time for eight years has been spent on this!"

I wondered what it was Joan Irvine Smith had picked up on those sun blistering trail rides with her grandfather that now pushed her into battle with half a hundred company executives and their lawyers. Few women, even those born into infinite wealth, have the combination of greed and gall to march into Congress and come away with the laws they need to build the future. Moreover, this extraordinary heiress and her septuagenarian lawyer were accumulating an image as public crusaders, a California-Electra version of Don Quixote and Sancho Panza.

I drove east down Memory Lane in search of the Santa Ana *Register*, where I would lose myself in old newspaper clippings. Foes of the Irvine Company seemed legion, all the way from the working-class city of Santa Ana, which lost a rich tax-base annexation fight with Irvine City, to the county human relations commission, which was blocked from inspecting an Irvine Company labor camp. All standard stuff in California.

Yet in the midst of all this squabbling over tax rights, human rights, and public nature sanctuaries, there appeared a clearly unusual Irvine potshotter, Max Sturges. A onetime southern California Goldwater chairman, right-wing opponent of fair housing, and former attorney to Bob Hope, seventy-year-old Sturges had leveled an amazing set of charges against the Irvine Company and its henchmen. The next morning at nine o'clock I drove out to see him.

Sturges's house is in one of the company's most stylish village communities called Big Canyon. A control booth and electric gate guard the entrance. Prim, with perfect posture, the gate assistant on duty handed me her clipboard and directed me to sign. Finished, I started to hand it back. "Oh, please note the time of arrival, sir." I did and drove my jeep up Chantilly Lane and around the corner to Rue St. Cloud.

I parked and before I could get to the apparently metal gate in front of Sturges's patio, he was there to greet me. No sooner had I sat down by his desk than he launched into the long list of threats he claimed to have received. Then he showed me the first piece of evidence, a long-bladed dagger with a firm handgrip made in Japan.

"My wife found that out in front of the garage one afternoon," he told me in a raspy voice, his finger waving at the knife. "She asked me what it meant."

"I asked her where it was lying. She told me.

"'That is a gangster's message for a hit,'" I told her. "'In other words, murder!'"

Sturges hadn't said that to the newspapers. Already I felt it was time to leave. But Sturges kept talking, mostly in starts and stops, pulling out maps and letters and pictures, setting his leather-sheathed dagger back in place so it would not collect any fingerprints. Pretty soon I realized he was running through a chronology beginning in 1971 when the Irvine Company had blocked him from building a house on a lot he had leased. The details of the squabble were not compelling, except that it had provoked him to wage a long and bloody fight with the company.

He explained how a woman introducing herself as an Irvine marketing researcher knocked on his door one morning, then asked him a lot of questions about his daily schedule, such as when he took his walks and where he went. The next morning, at exactly the time he had told her he would cross the main road in front of his subdivision, he said a speeding maroon pickup truck bore right toward him, forcing him to jump over with his knee braces on into the median.

Sturges kept on. I couldn't divert him for an instant from his chronology: from the fire next door that started while "a police helicopter hovered overhead," or the threatening phone call that came a week after the fire, warning, "We got the wrong house the other day, but we'll burn you out next time!" Or about the police beating he described getting, or the two people he remembers staring through his bedroom window one morning at 5:00 A.M.

Finally he finished. He sat quiet a moment and hobbled his way over to the window next to a bed piled full of papers. He brushed aside the thin white curtains. Underneath was a high-powered rifle. Beneath the curtains on the other side, a second. "I've been living in a fortress here," he declared. "I asked the sheriff's office for protection and I was refused, said they couldn't do it." He explained he couldn't go to the Newport Beach police since they allegedly had beaten him up.

"It's a police state we're living in here. There's no other way to describe it." He stopped and reminded me of the threatening phone call. Then he pulled the barrel of his rifle out from the wall. "You know what I told 'em? I said, 'I've still got a carbine I killed Japs with in New Guinea in 1944 and I'll have it loaded for you.' Then I hung up.''

A crotchety wheeler-dealer lawyer, a blonde heiress, alleged foundation fraud, and a heavy finger on a federal law: that seemed quite a lot. But Japanese daggers, loaded carbines, and mobster contracts? The story seemed to go too far. Suspicious that age and paranoia had gotten the better of Max Sturges's once flashy law practice, I asked him temperately, "But Mr. Sturges, what's the point of all this?"

"You just take your time and come over here," he ordered, laying out a map by the front window. Dutifully I came to look. His hand hovered over the map, and he stared me in the eye.

"A hundred million dollars in worthless land titles," he proclaimed.

"That's right, $100 million. All those houses down on Newport Bay, some of 'em worth $150,000 each, and the titles underneath are no good. That's why they don't want anybody snoopin' around!"

Max had me for another hour.

His case rambled on. He pulled out more photocopies of old survey maps, newspaper stories for the *Los Angeles Times*, court rulings half a century old, and historical descriptions of the original Spanish land-grants. The man had spent years sifting through the law libraries and public offices of southern California. Here he was, this strange shriveled human being, who claimed in an aside to have formed the first band with Glenn Miller and Benny Goodman, who today wanders around a frightfully tacky luxury house in a desert subdivision with French street names, and who wakes up every morning and goes to bed every night in continuous fear for his life. All because he stumbled onto a "realization" that the nation's biggest city builder had constructed millions of dollars of housing on land it possibly didn't own.

And who did own the land? I asked. "The public," he answered. All the luxury houses (one owned by H. R. Haldeman) that had been thrown up on man-made fill along the edge of the Bay, plus the man-made islands sagging alongside, he argued, were governed by century-old laws designed to protect tidelands for the public interest. Therefore, he insisted, since the land either didn't exist or was covered by tides at the time the law was written, it was public property, and neither the Irvine Company nor any of the homeowners could possibly have clear legal titles to it.

"Don't just trust me," Sturges said when he finished. "Go talk to this man here. Ted Parker. He's a law professor who's been studying it for the county. Has an office over at Western States Law School in Santa Ana."

On the way to Parker, I related Sturges's tale to my research associate, who had been immersing himself in old newspaper clippings. "Ah," he muttered. "I don't know about Sturges's and the *lower* bay titles, but . . . . " He began to recount an even more complicated story of how the Irvine Company had tried for years to trade three Upper Bay islands to the county in exchange for some publicly held frontage where it wanted to build a posh marina complex. Again there was serious question over whether Irvine had clear title to the lands it wanted to dispose of.

The perfect counterpoint to lawyers Sturges and Young, Ted Parker waited for us in a tiny professorial cubicle. "Oh yes, Max," he began. "You've got to watch Max. He comes up with the right answers, but for all the wrong reasons." As for the phony titles down on the Lower Bay, the roundish, friendly, graying professor Parker found Max's arguments complicated. But the other title issue, the Upper Bay islands Irvine wanted to trade, they were his specialty. And not just any specialty. They had caused a hot controversy, and his report to the county, he promised, would be about three feet thick and would recount the history of California tidelands law for the previous century and a quarter. For the moment we requested a condensed version, which ran about as follows.

The lands Irvine wanted to trade to the county, including three islands in the upper neck of Newport Bay, would be exchanged for prime water frontage to transform most of the bay into one large Irvine-operated marina. State law required that lands received by the public must be at least as valuable as those traded away. Opponents of the trade argued that not only would it essentially give Newport Bay to the Irvine Company, but that most company-offered shoreline was inaccessible to the water and the three islands were possibly worth nothing at all. The value of those islands was central to the issue; Irvine claimed they were worth $9 million. But, Professor Parker noted, that value depended upon whether Irvine could claim clear title to the islands, a judgment that reaches back to a nineteenth-century survey classifying the islands as "above the tide" and therefore available for private ownership.

If, however, as much of the evidence suggests, the islands were submerged during high tide as of 1850 when California entered the Union, then under a number of later court rulings the public is guaranteed the right of use and access to them—including fishing, swimming, navigation, and recreation. What it also means is that the islands are essentially worthless since the private owner, Irvine, would be prohibited from placing any commercial development on them.

And, therefore, the company would be offering a worthless trade, effectively charging the public $9 million for land it already had.

One irate citizen who was especially vociferous in opposing the land trade pointed out how the $9 million was a drop in the bucket for Irvine: "Irvine would gain title to 34,000 feet of prime waterfront property, and by creating artificial finger inlets and peninsulas, could increase this shoreline to 70,000 feet."[2] Since waterfront property was selling for an average of $2,500 per lineal foot at this time, the company stood to make $150 million profit through the trade.

A citizen campaign against the trade, culminating in a court judgment finally blocked the deal in January 1973. Now the Irvine Company has given up any hopes of developing the Upper Bay, quietly reversing ten years of heated battle and offering its three islands to any public agency willing to work out a "fair price." If the county supervisors should read Professor Parker's research to mean the islands are already in the public domain, then Irvine could be offered nothing for them. "If it were determined that the public had an easement to those lands, their market-value would be zero," one county attorney advised.

"The Irvines have felt like they were the great manorial lords of early England, that what was good for Irvine was good for the people," Parker chuckled as he would up his discourse on the controversy's legal intricacies.

The fight to preserve Newport's Upper Bay, it seemed, had been the Irvine Company's biggest defeat to date, a flat roadblock against what President Ray Watson called the "inevitability of growth." Moreover, it had happened simul-

2. Statement made during a personal interview in June 1974.

taneously with a political realignment of the county supervisors in which the company lost its historic rubber stamp approval for almost any new project. Parker admitted as much.
But when I asked him if the title questions surrounding the
Upper Bay fight didn't also support Max Sturges's claims
about flimsy titles in the Lower Bay, he became much more
cautious.

"The county's only interest is in resolving the Upper Bay
issue," he reassured me.

"Yes," I told him. "I understand, but hasn't this raised
serious issues about legal title to lands in the Lower Bay,
especially those covering land fill which didn't exist before
1900, much less before 1850? If Irvine saw the prospect of
litigation on those already developed lands, might it not decide that the best tactic would be to resolve the Upper Bay
controversy as quickly as possible in hopes that the entire
title issue would be forgotten?"

"Well," Parker agreed, "there could be an issue in the
Lower Bay, if it were shown that the developments there
were placed on man-made fill instead of on a natural extension of the shoreline. Then possibly somebody could argue
that those lands as well were governed by tidelands protection law, and well, if that were judged to be the case, possibly all those lands might be owned by the state, and not by
the homeowners or by Irvine."

"So all those deeds down there would be wiped out?" I
asked.

"That's hard to say," he answered. "There's still the
principle of possession as nine-tenths of the law. And anyway they'd change the Constitution first, before anything
like that happened. You've got to realize these are the guys
who finance and pay for the elections that you're talking

about. Nobody wants to look into those titles. Flournoy [the Republican candidate for governor] doesn't want those titles investigated. I just talked to him the other day. Neither does Jerry Brown [then the Democratic candidate]!"

"All those islands down in Newport Beach could be questionable, not just Irvine's. When it started they were all just shifting sandbars; big storms would blow in one year, and the next year they might not even be in the same place. Even today you go down there when the Chubasco blows in from the mountains and knocks those boats around. It'll let you know that mother nature still likes to have her way."

Just as I was about to leave Parker's office, I asked him what he thought of Max Sturges's stories about someone trying to get him. "Oh well, Max, uh . . . people have told me Irvine isn't above using strong arm tactics, but I don't think anybody'd want to hurt Max." We talked a moment longer, and I asked him how such a mild-toned professor had become involved in this fight. "Oh my father got me interested in helping the county get this settled. He used to play all over Newport Beach when he was a kid."

"Your father?"

"Yes, he's head of the First American Title Insurance Company."

I turned to Steve and asked him if he didn't think this story was beginning to get out of hand, if we weren't falling prey to too many knots and angles in this report about the nation's biggest city builder. He smiled, his eyes dancing with yet another new twist. Flipping through a fistful of Xeroxed newspaper clippings, he showed me one and began to read the highlights.

For all the years Irvine had pursued the land trade, he

summarized, it had also refused to pay taxes on the land under dispute—producing today a total tax liability of about $7 million including interest penalties. At first the county supervisors had directed that no assessments be made against the company. But, county tax assessor Andrew Hinshaw balked and declared he would assess Irvine its properly assessed rate—an almost unheard of action that gave a big boost to opponents of the land trade, and an action so unusual it helped propel Hinshaw into Congress four years later.

"So?" I remarked. "Lots of companies don't pay taxes. There must be honest property tax assessors even in California."

"I'm sure there are," Steve said. "But who do you think runs Hinshaw's office here in the county? Joan Irvine Smith's public relations man. Not only that, Joan was one of the biggest campaigners against the land trade."

> Once, a family decided to pack up their belongings, say goodbye to their friends, and move to southern California. Though they had heard about this place, and seen pictures of it, they didn't quite know what to expect. Movie stars? Freeways? Disneyland? It was hard leaving the old neighborhood. The old house. And as they shut the front door behind them for the very last time, they wondered: "Will we ever feel at home again?"
> —from *Welcome Home,* a boxed booklet
> of The Irvine Company

"Will we ever feel at home again?"

Irvine Company planners could have posed no better question for the multitudes of new residents they are bringing to Orange County. Company chieftains like Ray Watson leave no doubt about what the answer is; they spend thousands of dollars each week convincing people of the "homelike" village atmosphere of their new futuristic city. The booklet *Welcome Home* is one of the Company's slickest efforts at luring corporate citizens to the new city; it includes three sections, one entitled "A Village Way of Life," a second labeled "Your Tomorrow," and a third identified simply as "Heritage." Together they aim to sell Irvine as the alternative to rootlessness, fear, and alienation—those hallmarks of American urban living.

"How to live happily ever after," reads the bold type of a full-page newspaper ad for Irvine, whose slogan is "We're doing southern California the way it should be." Perhaps so. But after two years of casual observation, and two weeks of intense examination—the most intense one company PR man said he could recall—serious frays seemed to surface in the fabric of the good life. A bright, affable man like Ray Watson can talk for hours about the unparalleled opportunity of having 83,000 acres all to himself to develop without the confusion of competitiors mucking up his plans. (His enthusiasm was mirrored by the receptionist who told us not to worry about parking tickets in the lots. "After all," she said with a smile, "we own them.")

Watson can inspire a vision of smalltown American warmth when he talks about the score of "villages" he has constructed throughout the Irvine plan. But at least one sociologist at nearby University of California, Irvine, finds all Watson's euphoria about village concepts so much blather: "Look, all they're doing up there is building suburban tracts. So they've got greenbelts and village names. A lot of places do. But suburban tracts are suburban tracts, even when they're expensive."

For Max Sturges, too, the talk about trust and good feelings is more than slightly hollow. Perhaps he suffers from the paranoia that advancing age sometimes brings with it. But he is not just any smalltown kook; he has held responsible positions in state and local Republican party committees and maintained one of the area's most successful law firms—hardly a left-wing anarchist ecologist, as critics of the Irvine Company are often described. Perhaps all that has happened to Max Sturges is that he suffered the unfortunate fate of learning too much too fast, of being tantalized by a million-dollar sales pitch for the good life, and being tortured by the realization that beneath it lay a lot of fast hustlers for the fast buck, who themselves were in the midst of struggling for control over one of America's richest corporate empires.

All of Irvine at times seems too much, too grand, too superlative. The biggest new town in America. The biggest private ranch in America. The biggest industrial park in America, which, ironically, doesn't pay most of its employees enough to live there. Even the freeways reinforce the aura of bigness, for, as I quickly discovered, city streets and county roads are too small and ineffective to move people around; the only way to travel in Orange County is by freeway. For Ray Watson it is all enthralling. "We don't have 'downtown' and 'suburbs' anymore," he declared. "L. A. people come over here to the beach in an hour, and I can drive over there to the symphony. It's really all just one big city." He failed to mention the three-pound, $16 book of street maps it takes to navigate through his "city."

Even the language the company uses possesses a certain grotesque grandeur, a kind of semi-English that struggles to establish parity between the gargantuan jargon and the gargantuan sums of money changing hands. "The city of Irvine should be people, and it should be all kinds of people. The city of Irvine should be a city—a distinctly urban form—

which provides residents the opportunity to express themselves through a multiplicity of life-styles. The city of Irvine
should be a definite place, for those who live there and for
those who visit, pass by, or only know of it by reputation."

Surely there is some silent unraveling of the senses when
words like those pass for a description of advanced city
planning. What stage of advance are we in when those in
charge write phrases like "cities are for people" and that
they must have locations?

My company host raised the same question in a slightly
different way. Touring us through Irvine's model village,
Eastbluff—the one he said city planners from around the
world come to visit and marvel over—he parked his car and
walked out to the Greenbelt, a long closely trimmed stretch
of flowers and grass running along the back sides of the
houses.

"Where do people put out their gardens?" I asked.

"Oh, uh, well I guess they could do it over there," he
stammered, pointing to a square yard of dirt between a tree
and a house.

"Hmm," I remarked. "Is it usually this quiet, so empty
on the Greenbelt at six o'clock in the afternoon?"

"Yeah," he answered. "Well I don't know, I drive
around with the, uh, groups out here, and umm, it's a funny
thing, where are all the people. I really don't know. I guess
maybe they're inside watching television or somethin'."

As living, breathing people replace the model people Irvine planners describe, they seem to be raising the same
question. Last spring the city of Irvine, which covers most
of the company's planned development, made national head-
lines with yet another "biggest." This time it was the biggest
drug bust in California history. Over 100 kids were pulled

out of their own or their parents' homes just as the sun began to sink into the sea.

Irvine, more than one knowledgeable source told me, had become the biggest drug market in Orange County, maybe even in the state. As the cases came to court, teen-agers began to talk about life in this immaculate, manicured city of the future. "This is really a bland community—middle-class, pretty, but it doesn't have any excitement, unless you are a sports hero," one said. "That's the only way a kid can get status, that and doing dope." One adult characterized Irvine's boredom as "the kind of feeling of helplessness that is found just as much in the adults and which is passed down from parents to their kids. It is the feeling you get when you have a beautiful house in Irvine, all the material things you have worked for, and your life still seems meaningless."

The kids described their lives as a compulsive search for thrills. One boasted that given a six-second start, he could dart in and out among the greenbelts and houses fast enough to lose anybody. He claimed he could run a block just along the imitation Spanish-style rooftops.

With no place to hang out but the supermarkets and the laundromats, many kids seem to gravitate toward the greenbelts, or at least toward the shrubs alongside where they can have a joint in private. But that has problems too.

"Everybody lives in a house that looks out on the greenbelt," Irvine city Mayor Gabby Pryor told one reporter. "You can't help but be aware of what is going on out there. You know who is making trouble."

"But will having a bust make any difference?" I asked her. "Will that stop kids from loitering on the greenbelt and smoking dope?"

"I could care less what they do in the privacy of their own

homes," she replied, obviously upset by the whole affair. "That's their business and that's their parents' business, but when they start being obnoxious in public and urinating on the bushes and defecating on the greenbelts or shouting 'Fuck You' to every passing adult or careening around on the sidewalks on their motorcycles, then they're going to be stopped.

"If we continue to get these kinds of parties where the kids are getting drunk or stoned or high, whatever, then . . . .They're overdosing. And they're lying in the gutters now when they overdose. There was a thirteen-year-old who was in the gutter two days ago of an overdose, and the neighbors found him and took him to the hospital and had to call the police in. Two weeks ago there were two seventeen-year-olds, one passed out, and they couldn't find a pulse on him. So they sent the emergency rescue out, and picked up the other kid who proceeded to beat up the policeman, so he had to be hospitalized. They had to call in a second car to get that kid; they handcuffed him and put him in a straight-jacket, then got the overdosed kid to a hospital and kept him alive.

"Now that is the type of thing the sixteen- and seventeen-year-old kids are doing, and I don't think it's a bit funny. So if it takes another drug bust to stop that kind of thing, then we'll keep on having them until those kids cut it out."

"And that," the company's *Welcome* brochure explains, "is why our villages were developed. To give you a place that still preserves the pleasure, the quiet harmony, and the good things all of us need in our lives."

Irvine is a planned community.

Appendix A
Tilling for Taxes: A Note on Income Shelters

Tax advantage is the reason many large investors, either corporations or individuals, enter "agribusiness" farming. By taking advantage of farm-related income shelter provisions in the tax law, they are able to avoid paying taxes on much of their regular income and obtain a good return on investment when they decide to sell their farm interest. Because the tax laws enable some kinds of capital investments to be separated from other kinds, it is possible for a rich investor with a high income to put some of his money into a farming venture that will be almost certain to "lose" money for the first few years of its existence. Then the investor can deduct these losses from his other income and thereby reduce the total amount of taxes he has to pay. That investment is called a *tax* or *income shelter* because it shelters or protects a part of his income from taxation.

The standard way such tax shelters work is for a group of investors to form an "investment syndicate" that then buys a portion of the farm's capital operations, such as newly planted vines and fruit trees that will take several years to produce any income. The investor, however, will not buy title to the land. In that way he is guaranteed an almost certain loss, or lack of income, for the first several nonproducing years of his operation. The result is that for all the years he is running a loss on his investment, he is actually able to make money by applying the amount of his loss against his other taxable income; the amount he has not had to pay in taxes on other income is the money he had made.

Law professor Charles Davenport at the University of California, Davis, offers an example of how the syndication works. Say you are representing a group of investors who together have $16 million. With that $16 million you buy equity in a new citrus orchard (i.e., your investors have "bought" the young trees planted in the orchard). In addition to the $16 million, the orchard obtains another $27 million from institutional lenders. Interest on the loan, arranged at very low rates before the current increases, after five years of operation would come to another $7 million. Total cost at the end of five years: $50 million. Meanwhile revenues during those early times would come to only $20 million, thereby producing a projected loss to the syndicated owners of $30 million. What could the syndicate do?

With figures as high as these, it's fair to assume the syndicate members are in a high-tax bracket, say, 70 percent. They subtract that $30 million loss from their own expected income. Since they would have expected to pay 70 percent tax on the $30 million in regular income, they have therefore saved $21 million. Discounting the future savings back to the present (sort of like figuring reverse interest) the syndicators can calculate that their loss has a present value of $18 million.

Let's say, in addition, the syndicators expect after five years to sell their farm interest. Will taxes on the sale cancel

out the value of their savings from the "loss"? Hardly. Let's
further assume they are not greedy and are willing to sell at
cost, for the $30 million which the operation lost, thereby
breaking even. Since the syndicators held their property for
several years, they can expect to take advantage of the long-
term "capital gains" tax rate; under capital gains tax only
half the sale value is taxed. Therefore only $15 million of the
sale will be taxable; at the 70 percent rate that comes to a tax
liability of $10.5 million, which discounted to its present
value (at the time of farm purchase) comes to $7.8 million.
So, in order to calculate the present tax savings for their
loss, the syndicators need only to subtract their present discounted tax liability from their present discounted tax savings. Of the $18 million value in tax savings available at
purchase, the present value of their tax burden is only $7.8
million—a savings of $10.2 million for their participation in
"farming." And that, of course, is on top of their initial $16
million which they get back in selling the property. That
means their $16 million is able to earn the equivalent (in
savings elsewhere) of $10.2 million in the deal, or about 12.7
percent a year. That is probably twice what the syndicators
could earn on standard stock investments, had they put their
$16 million on the exchange. And it is certainly better than
they could have gotten from federal Treasury notes. Of
course, this does come from the federal Treasury too—in
taxes not paid. One estimate is that the special accounting
rules permitting such sheltered investment costs the United
States taxpayer over $800 million a year.

Even more serious for American farming is that these tax
rules enable such large syndicate "farmers" to operate on
invisible margins since farming is only a means of cancelling
out profits made elsewhere. They, therefore, have an extraor-

dinary advantage over real farmers who have no such outside income and who must depend on the actual farm product for a living. Since the tax shelter scheme encourages new entries into farming, it may well be that the eventual consequence of these large new outfits is a temporary glutting of the market accompanied by a depression in wholesale prices. Furthermore, the large syndicated producer not dependent upon commodity prices for his survival is able to capture more and more of the market by selling at breakeven or loss prices, which for the above described tax reasons may be beneficial to the syndicate investors. Such lower prices may seem advantageous to the consumer. These conditions, however, are a prime element in driving out the independent, marginal producers who have no other income to depend upon. As that happens more and more, then agriculture is increasingly left to monopoly growers who in the future will be able to set their own prices. And after the tax advantages are gone, there is no reason to assume any investors will want to keep prices down, especially when they are freed of competitor pressure. In that way tax law tends to discourage diversified, independent farming and farm ownership while at the same time assuring even higher food prices in the future.

Appendix B

TABLE 1

Agricultural and Nonagricultural Uses of Land, United States, 1969

Major Land Use	Acreage	Percentage of Total
	Million acres	Percentage
Agricultural:		
Cropland	472	20.9
Cropland used for crops[1]	(333)	(14.7)
Soil improvement crops and idle cropland	(51)	(2.3)
Cropland pasture	(88)	(3.9)
Grassland pasture and range[2]	604	26.7
Forest land grazed	198	8.7
Farmsteads, farm roads	9	.4
Total agricultural land	1,283	56.7
Nonagricultural:		
Forest land not grazed[3]	525	23.2
Special uses	169	7.5
Urban and other built-up areas[4]	(61)	(2.7)
Primarily for recreation and wildlife[5]	(81)	(3.6)
Public installations and facilities[6]	(27)	(1.2)
Miscellaneous land[7]	287	12.6
Total nonagricultural land	981	43.3
Total land area	2,264	100.0

Source: "Major Uses of Land in the United States: Summary Report for 1969," U.S. Dept. of Agriculture, Agricultural Economic Report No. 247, Economic Research Service, p. 2.

[1] Cropland harvested, crop failure, and cultivated summer fallow.
[2] Excludes cropland used only for pasture.
[3] Excludes reserved and other forest land duplicated in parks and other special use areas. It was not feasible to eliminate all overlap that exists because of multiple use.
[4] Urban areas; highway, road, and railroad rights-of-way; and airports.
[5] National and State parks and related recreational areas, national and State wildlife refuges, and national forest wilderness and primitive areas.
[6] Federal land administered by the Department of Defense and the Atomic Energy Commission, and State land in institutional and miscellaneous special uses.
[7] Includes miscellaneous uses not inventoried, and areas of little use such as marshes, open swamps, bare rock areas, desert, and tundra.
Estimates are based primarily on reports and records of the Bureau of the Census and Federal and State land management and conservation agencies.

TABLE 2

Percentage Distribution of the Number of Farms and Land in the United States, 1969[1]

	Business Organizations									
	Distribution of Number of Farms					Distribution of Land in Farms				
			Corporations					Corporations		
			Shareholders					Shareholders		
Region	Individual	Partnership	10 or less	Over 10	Total	Individual	Partnership	10 or less	Over 10	Total
	Percentage					Percentage				
Northeast	87.2	10.5	1.7	0.1	1.8	81.9	13.7	3.3	0.6	3.9
Lake States	87.3	11.7	0.5	0.1	0.6	83.3	14.6	1.4	0.3	1.7
Corn Belt	84.4	14.3	0.6	0.1	0.7	80.3	17.7	1.3	0.1	1.4
Northern Plains	86.7	12.1	0.6	[2]	0.6	80.1	16.2	2.8	0.3	3.1
Appalachian	83.9	14.5	1.0	0.1	1.1	78.2	18.3	2.3	0.5	2.8
Southeast	85.0	11.7	2.4	0.2	2.6	71.0	15.2	8.7	3.9	12.6
Delta States	86.0	11.7	1.5	0.2	1.7	74.0	18.3	5.4	1.6	7.0
Southern Plains	87.0	11.4	0.7	0.1	0.8	72.8	19.6	4.2	1.6	5.8
Mountain	83.2	12.7	3.3	0.2	3.5	60.1	18.2	18.0	2.8	20.8
Pacific	83.1	12.9	2.9	0.3	3.2	62.4	21.1	[3]11.1	[3]3.6	15.4
U.S. Total	85.4	12.8	1.1	0.1	1.2	72.5	17.8	[3]7.2	[3]1.6	8.8

Source: 1969 Census of Agriculture—County Data. Table 12. U.S. Dept. of Commerce.
[1] Does not show percentage of "other" business organizations, farms with $2,500 or more.
[2] Less than .05 percent.
[3] Excludes Alaska.

TABLE 3

Number of Farms and Land in Farms in the United States, 1969[1]

| Region | Business Organizations — Number of Farms | | | | | Business Organizations — Land in Farms | | | | |
	Individual	Partnership	Corporations Shareholders 10 or less	Corporations Shareholders Over 10	Corporations Total	Individual	Partnership	Corporations Shareholders 10 or less	Corporations Shareholders Over 10	Corporations Total
	Numbers					Thousand Acres				
Northeast	96,914	11,711	1,874	115	1,989	19,201	3,210	773	136	909
Lake States	183,498	24,544	1,168	138	1,306	42,914	7,544	695	166	861
Corn Belt	374,738	63,726	2,664	254	2,918	91,237	20,773	1,490	184	1,675
Northern Plain	185,429	25,946	1,241	105	1,346	137,723	27,812	4,764	584	5,348
Appalachian	176,748	30,514	2,061	154	2,215	32,364	7,577	950	197	1,141
Southeast	88,995	12,236	2,564	204	2,768	28,727	6,145	3,527	1,598	5,125
Delta States	69,522	9,491	1,179	175	1,354	24,308	6,010	1,777	507	2,284
Southern Plains	150,138	19,607	1,243	153	1,396	117,071	31,767	6,930	2,552	9,482
Mountain	75,380	11,462	3,000	185	3,158	125,454	38,076	37,489	5,908	43,397
Pacific	79,203	12,298	2,723	314	3,037	42,795	14,474	7,605[2]	2,478[2]	10,083
U.S. Total	1,480,565	221,535	19,717	1,797	21,514	665,693	163,388	66,000	14,310	80,310

Source: 1969 Census of Agriculture—County Data, Table 12, U.S. Dept. of Commerce.
[1] Farms with sales of $2,500 or more.
[2] Excludes Alaska.

TABLE 4

Ownership Characteristics of Farm Operators

Type	Percentage of All Farms	Average Number of Acres	Percentage of All Land in Farms	Average Value Products Sold	Percentage Value Products Sold
Full owners[1]	62	220	35	$10,869	41
Part owners[2]	25	820	52	$29,775	44
Tenants[3]	13	390	13	$20,024	15

Source: 1969 Census of Agriculture, U.S. Dept. of Commerce.
[1] Operators who operate only land they own.
[2] Operators who operate land they own and also land they rent.
[3] Operators who operate only land they rent.

TABLE 5

Area of Commercial Timberland in the United States by Ownership and Region: 1952, 1962, 1970
(Thousand Acres)

| Region | Year | All Owner-ships | Total Public | Federal | | | | | State | County and Munic-ipal | Total Private | Private | | |
				Total Federal	National Forest	Bureau of Land Manage-ment	Indian	Miscel-laneous Federal				Forest Industry	Farmer	Miscel-laneous Private
New England	1970	32,367	1,993	911	832	0	0	79	775	306	30,374	9,988	3,637	16,748
	1962	31,878	1,811	906	831	0	0	75	624	281	30,067	8,104	5,635	16,328
	1952	30,935	1,741	904	810	0	0	94	580	257	29,194	8,178	7,842	13,174
Middle Atlantic	1970	49,685	5,796	1,500	1,367	0	0	133	3,890	405	43,888	2,454	9,907	31,526
	1962	46,737	5,708	1,538	1,319	0	0	219	3,890	280	41,029	2,229	12,072	26,728
	1952	42,098	5,514	1,541	1,335	0	0	206	3,645	328	36,584	1,965	15,114	19,505
Lake States	1970	50,840	20,556	7,059	5,867	74	804	312	7,723	5,774	30,284	4,438	11,694	14,151
	1962	51,530	20,936	7,451	5,923	80	1,096	351	7,553	5,932	30,593	3,195	13,360	14,037
	1952	52,604	21,812	7,818	5,962	65	1,281	509	7,637	6,356	30,792	3,068	14,631	13,092
Central	1970	45,008	3,565	2,840	2,390	0	10	438	686	39	41,442	681	25,778	14,982
	1962	44,942	3,299	2,552	2,196	0	8	347	674	71	41,642	688	27,304	13,649
	1952	44,559	3,273	2,699	2,208	1	6	483	529	45	41,285	817	28,848	11,620

Region	Year													
South	1970	192,542	17,278	14,277	10,764	11	219	3,282	2,321	680	175,263	35,325	65,136	74,801
	1962	199,905	17,177	14,274	10,689	26	229	3,329	2,217	686	182,727	34,069	73,174	75,484
	1952	192,082	16,806	14,295	10,405	161	242	3,486	1,854	656	175,276	32,055	91,311	51,908
Pacific Northwest	1970	49,713	30,646	27,070	22,571	2,377	1,942	180	3,269	307	19,067	9,554	4,716	4,797
	1962	50,407	31,956	27,648	22,883	2,629	1,982	154	3,076	332	19,351	9,471	5,120	4,760
	1952	50,580	31,364	28,003	22,115	2,954	2,809	125	2,892	469	19,225	9,046	5,406	4,773
Pacific Southwest	1970	17,909	9,315	8,751	8,314	275	102	30	559	5	8,593	2,665	1,885	4,042
	1962	18,132	9,420	8,859	8,393	303	114	49	558	3	8,712	2,457	1,964	4,291
	1952	18,216	9,571	8,883	8,372	318	144	49	680	8	8,645	2,167	2,030	4,448
Rocky Mountain	1970	61,631	46,968	44,699	39,787	2,024	2,809	78	2,197	71	14,663	2,233	8,379	4,050
	1962	64,603	49,895	47,619	42,692	2,030	2,817	78	2,204	71	14,708	2,249	8,404	4,051
	1952	63,891	49,120	46,834	41,886	2,038	2,830	79	2,214	71	14,771	2,256	8,440	4,080
Total All Regions	1970	499,697	136,120	107,108	91,924	4,761	5,888	4,534	21,422	7,588	363,576	67,341	131,134	165,100
	1962	598,137	139,304	110,819	94,927	5,068	6,248	4,604	20,797	7,657	368,833	62,455	147,035	169,342
	1952	494,978	139,202	110,973	93,094	5,538	7,313	5,032	20,032	8,191	355,775	59,547	173,624	122,654

Source: U.S. Forest Service, Dept. of Agriculture.

TABLE 6

Public Outdoor Recreation Acreage by Type of Area and Administering Jurisdiction, 1972[1]

(Thousand Acres)

Administering Jurisdiction	Total	Regional, Community, and Neighborhood Parks and Recreation Areas	Forest Areas	Fish and Game Areas	Historic and Cultural Areas	Wilderness, Primitive, and Natural Areas	Other
Federal	266,719.9	19,106.8	160,165.1	32,789.9	1,310.8	28,094.8	25,252.5
State	41,794.5	4,412.4	19,058.2	15,771.4	49.4	1,432.2	1,070.9
County	8,131.5	1,298.8	4,047.9	1,406.7	11.3	1,338.2	28.6
City	1,629.1	697.4	383.2	209.6	7.5	232.0	99.4
Township	631.4	74.0	495.5	38.3	0.9	21.8	0.9
Park and recreation districts and regional councils	336.1	166.9	9.9	45.0	2.0	94.1	18.2
Total	319,242.5	25,756.3	184,159.8	50,260.9	1,381.9	31,213.1	26,470.5

[1] Table based on reports received from individual agencies administering recreation lands within each governmental jurisdiction. Data include only land primarily used for public outdoor recreation purposes. Federal data were reported by the National Park Service, Bureau of Land Management, Bureau of Sport Fisheries and Wildlife, Bureau of Reclamation, Forest Service, Corps of Engineers and Tennessee Valley Authority. The inventory included all State agencies, counties, cities with over 5,000 population, townships with greater than 25,000 population, park and recreation districts and regional councils. Cities with less than 5,000 population and townships with less than 25,000 population were sampled and expanded to reflect the total universe. Both sample and nonsampled data were adjusted for nonreported values. Due to rounding, figures may not total.

TABLE 7

Private Outdoor Recreation, 1975

Geographic Division	Number of Enterprises	Acreage			
		Total	Land	Water	Wetland
U.S. Total	131,849	30,025,200	28,845,097	1,038,807	141,296
New England	6,564	763,557	707,992	41,194	14,371
Middle Atlantic	17,139	968,624	916,325	23,100	29,199
East North Central	26,149	1,320,929	1,121,737	161,168	38,024
West North Central	14,021	2,340,642	2,248,181	91,253	1,208
South Atlantic	20,849	1,248,749	1,036,863	164,622	47,264
East South Central	3,976	308,746	283,969	24,092	685
West South Central	19,111	14,692,845	14,500,482	184,191	8,172
Mountain	10,974	5,623,056	5,450,887	172,020	149
Pacific	13,066	2,758,052	2,578,661	177,167	2,224

Source: Selected Outdoor Recreation Statistics, Bureau of Outdoor Recreation, Dept. of Interior (1971).

TABLE 8

Number of Filings, Lots, and Acres in
Recreational Land Filings Registered with the
U.S. Office of Interstate Land Sales (HUD), by Region, 1974

Region	Number of Registered Filings	Number of Lots in Registered Filings	Number Acres in Registered Filings
United States	5,498	3,375,821	7,146,229
Northeastern	444	133,671	231,555
New England	(202)	(36,766)	(77,251)
Mid Atlantic	(242)	(96,905)	(154,304)
North Central	634	244,886	279,214
East North Central	(354)	(132,389)	(168,634)
West North Central	(280)	(92,497)	(110,580)
South	2,518	2,037,908	3,370,140
South Atlantic	(1,354)	(1,113,146)	(2,243,119)
East South Central	(282)	(123,022)	(127,291)
West South Central	(882)	(801,740)	(999,730)
West	1,902	979,356	3,265,320
Mountain	(1,253)	(750,270)	(2,489,408)
Pacific	(649)	(229,086)	(775,912)

Source: Dept. of Housing and Urban Development.

TABLE 9

Acres in Recreational Land Filings
Registered With U.S. Office of Interstate Land Sales
Ranking of States with at least One Percent of Total Acres, 1974

State	Total Acres in Registered Filings	Percentage Total Acres in Registered Filings in United States	Cumulative Percentage
1. Florida	1,942,155	27.0	27.0
2. New Mexico	1,030,208	14.4	41.4
3. Texas	876,390	12.3	53.7
4. Colorado	824,700	11.5	65.2
5. California	622,329	8.7	73.9
6. Arizona	467,015	6.5	80.4
7. Pennsylvania	135,435	1.9	82.3
8. Arkansas	101,449	1.4	83.7
9. North Carolina	92,204	1.3	85.0
10. Virginia	85,303	1.2	86.2
11. Nevada	70,208	1.0	87.2
12. Hawaii	67,944	1.0	88.2

Source: Dept. of Housing and Urban Development.

TABLE 10
Federal Lands Disposal by Agency

Agency	Acreage	Types	Mode of Disposal
Forest Service	186,000,000	Forest products Minerals Forage	Lease Lease or sale Lease
Bureau of Land Management	475,000,000	Forest products Minerals Forage Land	Lease Lease or sale Lease Grant, sales, some permits
National Park Service	25,000,000	All uses	No sale, lease or permits
Fish and Wildlife Service	28,000,000	All uses	No sale—certain resources may be leased
Defense Dept.	30,000,000	Defense uses	No sales—unless surplus

Source: Information compiled by Congressional Research Service, Library of Congress, from relevant agencies.

TABLE 11

Mineral and Petroleum Leases on Public Lands[1]

Minerals			
Land Category and Minerals	Producible Mines	Number Leases	Acreage
Public			
Coal	63	767	1,419,248
Phosphate	10	161	121,978
Potash	12	188	285,065
Sodium	13	112	175,942
Other	7	49	16,239
Total	105	1,277	2,018,472
Acquired lands	17	277	281,267
Indian lands	216	1,025	5,266,701
Total Minerals	338	2,579	7,566,440
Oil and Gas			
Public		94,379	67,673,530
Acquired lands		9,898	6,659,463
Indian lands		9,904	3,550,191
Total		114,181	77,883,184
Continental Shelf		1,096	4,688,739
Total oil and gas		115,277	82,571,923

Source: Data as of June 30, 1973, Geological Survey, "Federal and Indian Lands, Coal, Phosphate, Potash, Sodium, and Other Mineral Production, Royalty Income, and Related Statistics," Dept. of Interior, May 1974.

[1] Does not include Osage Nation, 2,559 oil and gas leases, 503,084.

TABLE 12

Federally Owned Land in the United States, June 30, 1973

Agency	Urban Acres	Rural Acres	Total
Atomic Energy Commission	45,109.6	2,057,394.3	2,102,503.9
Central Intelligence Agency	213.1	95.6	308.7
Dept. of Commerce	670.6	57,305.3	57,975.9
Dept. of Justice	3,798.6	24,159.3	27,957.9
Dept. of Labor	3,759.6	0	3,759.6
Dept. of State	349.4	122,245.3	122,594.7
Dept. of Agriculture	1,940.9	187,626,757.6	187,628,698.5
Dept. of Health, Education and Welfare	3,169.7	892.4	4,062.1
Dept. of Housing and Urban Development	5.7	2.7	8.4
Dept. of Interior	67,537.3	539,085,788.6	539,153,325.9
Dept. of Transport.	10,889.9	160,198.9	171,088.5
Environmental Protection Agency	190.0	59.5	249.5
Federal Communications Commissions	10.0	2,646.3	2,646.3
General Services Administration	13,579.9	6,656.1	20,236.0
Government Printing Office	5.5	0.0	5.5
National Science Foundation	570.2	3,151.0	3,721.2
NASA	4,648.0	132,427.1	137,075.1
National Capital Housing Authority	1.8	0.0	1.8
Office of Economic Opportunity	8.6	51.8	60.4
Tennessee Valley Authority	166.2	915,959.0	916,125.2
Treasury Dept.	27.6	408.2	435.8
U.S. Information Agency	0.0	8,701.9	8,701.9
U.S. Postal Service	2,113.5	0.0	2,113.5
Veterans Administration	11,625.2	7,751.5	19,376.7

(continued)

TABLE 12
(continued)

Federally Owned Land in the United States, June 30, 1973

Agency	Urban Acres	Rural Acres	Total
Total civil agencies	170,380.9	730,212,652.1	730,383,033.0
Defense Agencies			
Dept. of Army	816,042.0	10,208,925.0	11,024,967.0
Dept. of Navy	1,768,681.7	1,793,458.1	3,562,139.8
Dept. of Air Force	46,950.0	8,340,390.0	8,387,340.0
Corps of Engineers	57,907.6	7,583,785.9	7,641,693.5
Total defense	2,689,581.3	27,926,559.0	30,616,140.3
Total all federal agencies	2,859,962.2	758,139,211.1	760,999,173.3

Source: "Inventory Report on Real Property Owned by the United States Throughout the World," June 30, 1973, General Services Administration.